Golf a la Carte®

Recipes from America's Finest Clubs

The Southeast

Edited By
James Y. Bartlett and D.G. Stern
Culinary Editor: Michele Ritter

NEPTUNE PRESS

WWW.GOLFCOOKBOOK.COM

Design and layout by Susan A. Bartlett, Caleb Clarke and James Y. Bartlett.

Library of Congress Control Number: 2008927386

Second North American Edition
ISBN: 978-0-9754676-3-3
Printed in Republic of Korea
Published by Neptune Press
Gladding House
Newport, Rhode Island 02840

Visit us at www.golfcookbook.com

Foreword

This is a new experience, the first time I've been asked to introduce a new cookbook. Food and golf do go together like hamburgers and buns, but my expertise is more in golf balls than meat balls, tee shots than crock pots, sand wedges than lemon wedges, well-hit drives than sour cream and chives. Not that I don't have a serious interest in good food.

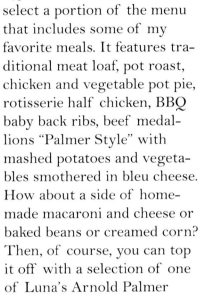

A long time ago (1959 for those keeping score) I arrived in Augusta, Georgia as the defending Masters champion. One of my duties was to select the menu for the annual Champion's Dinner, held Tuesday evening of Masters Week and attended by the club's Chairman and every former winner.

Some champions like to get fancy with the menu selection and others opt for regional specialties from the places they live. Me? I decided to keep it simple: a choice of steak or chicken.

I relish a good meal as much as anybody, at home, at the club or in a restaurant. But my personal tastes in food are fairly simple. Meat and potatoes. Roasted chicken. Still, I insist that the food and beverage service at my country clubs in Florida and Pennsylvania be top notch in all aspects. I think it speaks well for my Bay Hill Club in Orlando that the editors of this book have selected three recipes of our fine chef, Robert Lee.

In my only venture into the commercial restaurant business—Arnold Palmer's Restaurant in La Quinta, California—I helped select a portion of the menu that includes some of my favorite meals. It features traditional meat loaf, pot roast, chicken and vegetable pot pie, rotisserie half chicken, BBQ baby back ribs, beef medallions "Palmer Style" with mashed potatoes and vegetables smothered in bleu cheese. How about a side of homemade macaroni and cheese or baked beans or creamed corn? Then, of course, you can top it off with a selection of one of Luna's Arnold Palmer wines. Not bad, eh?

My tastes may not be overly fancy, but over the years I have learned one thing: the men and women who work in the kitchens at my clubs and restaurant are true professionals at what they do. Some days they have to prepare a meal for a couple hundred wedding guests, and other days it's a romantic candlelight dinner for two. The country club chef is an often overlooked part of a club's success.

They work wonders every day in the kitchen and I tip my hat to every one of them.

Arnold Palmer
Arnold Palmer's Bay Hill Club and Lodge

Introduction

It is with great professional pride that I write this introduction to *Golf a la Carte: Recipes from America's Finest Clubs.* As the Executive Chef of the prestigious East Lake Golf Club in Atlanta, Georgia, I understand the importance of providing great cuisine to our memberships.

The club experience—having every need catered to while playing on a fantastic course—is the ultimate for a golfer. And enjoying a wonderful meal is part of that experience.

Be it a perfectly cooked hamburger before one's round begins, or sitting at a business dinner with one's peers in the clubhouse after a great outing, the food will be remembered long after the memories of the round have faded away.

The chefs in this cookbook put their professionalism, hearts and souls out there daily for everyone to see. They have spent years working on their craft, learning the techniques and adjusting their flavor profiles to fit their memberships perfectly. Just as golfers make adjustments on each course they play; professional chefs must make similar adjustments in their kitchens, based upon their membership's profile.

As President of one of the largest chapters in the American Culinary Federation, with more than 800 members in the Atlanta chapter, I truly understand the philosophy of taking care of one's membership. The ACF is the professional voice of food in America and is responsible for the certification and education of many fine club chefs. These chefs pursue a higher standard of professionalism through certification all the way up to Certified Master Chef.

This cookbook will give you unprecedented look into the soul of a golf club chef through their favorite recipes. In presenting them, these chefs would like to share a part of themselves not only with those who read and adapt these recipes, but fellow chefs from all over the world.

I would be remiss if I did not thank the publishers of *Golf a la Carte* for their continued support of not only the chefs who work in the golf arena, but for also investing the time and resources that this project required.

By doing so, *Golf a la Carte* has let the enthusiastic culinary public know that some of the best chefs in the world practice their amazing craft at great golf clubs all over the world.

Michael Deihl, CEC CCA AAC
Executive Chef
East Lake Golf Club

Table of Contents

Appetizers

Lunch & Salads

TABLE OF CONTENTS

Sauces, Dressings & Sides

Soups & Stews

Entrees
Meat Dishes

Pasta, Poultry & More

TABLE OF CONTENTS

Desserts

The Pick of the Pros
Rating the wines of the Tour's best

Once upon a time, a successful Touring pro reaching the end of his career might be expected to try his hand at designing golf courses or marketing a line of golf clubs. These days, however, a growing number of old pros—and even a few young ones—are instead stomping on grapes and worrying about botrytis attacking their cabernets.

Well, OK, maybe Arnold Palmer himself isn't out there toiling in the vineyards where the grapes of wrath are stored, but he does have his signature on a bottle. As do Ernie Els, Mike Weir, David Frost, Greg Norman and even the PGA Tour it's own-self. Somewhere along the line, somebody has decided that wine and golf go together as smoothly as "double" and "bogey."

Golf pros, of course, have long tried to translate their prowess on the fairways into other kinds of business ventures. Jack Nicklaus has made and lost a couple of fortunes in business deals off-course, which may be one reason that the Golden Bear hasn't yet come out with his own vintages. Arnold Palmer started this whole golfer-as-international-conglomerate thing, and one can only hope he's kept the Pennzoil well removed from the wine-bottling machines. Tiger Woods, who makes millions for just smiling into the camera, has yet to launch a vineyard inasmuch as he's pretty busy being the best golfer in

the world.

So while we're sure there may be more golfing vintages before long, we decided it was time to gather up some of the birdie Bordeaux, the sauvignon shank, the pros' plonk and see if any of it is any good.

The scorecard:

Engelbrecht Els Vineyard

South African star Els joined forces with an old friend, Jean Engelbrecht, to launch a vineyard in the Stellenbosch region in 2004. Els says he prefers rich Bordeaux reds, while Engelbrecht is more of a shiraz fan, so many of their wines contain a little of both.

We sampled the 2002 Ernie Els Stellenbosch ($90), which contains 61% cabernet sauvignon, 24% merlot, and a few dashes of malbec, cab franc and petit verdot. It had a nice, earthy aroma when first opened, which only got deeper and richer as the wine opened up. Dark, fruity tastes and a lot of tannin told us that this was a wine that should go on the shelf for a few years to age. We'll bet this would make an excellent wine for Christmas dinner in, oh, 2010 or so.

We also tried the Engelbrecht Els 2003 ($50), with 21 % shiraz added to mostly cab sauvignon. This one also had a good nose, with notes of berries, licorice and sun, a nice mouth feel and some complexity that lasted to the finish, when the spicy shiraz kicked in with hints of green pepper.

This would be a good picnic wine for summer.

Greg Norman Estates

The Great White Shark has been making wine in his native Australia for at least a decade now, and recently added some Californian vineyards to his collection.

Working with Foster's Wine Estates, formerly Beringer Blass, and hiring Ron Schrieve as his winemaker, Norman currently offers five different California vintages: a chardonnay and a pinot noir from Santa Barbara, a petit sirah from Paso Robles, a Lake County zinfandel, and a North Coast cabernet sauvignon. All of these vintages from 2003 and 2004 are priced at around $18.

We opened up the North Coast cabernet sauvignon and inhaled the flavors of blueberries and black currants. Muted tannins kept the wine alive until late notes of mint and sweet oak—no doubt from the aging barrels—chimed in. The wine has a short finish, but it's quite enjoyable.

Being big syrah/shiraz fans, we looked forward to the Greg Norman Petit Sirah. And while the wine opened nicely, with flavors of tobacco, chocolate, blackberries and vanilla on the nose, the nice rusticity didn't last long enough. The finish, alas, petered out. Kind of like, said an unkind observer, the Shark's Sunday round at the '96 Masters.
He must have been one of the millions to have lost some bets that sad day.

Arnold Palmer Wines

Arnie hitched his wine wagon to Mike Moone's Luna Vineyards in Napa in 2003 and so far they've brought out two varieties: a cabernet

sauvignon and a chardonnay. Each is priced at around $15.

With a chicken roasting in the oven, we opened the '03 Chardonnay. It had a lovely citrus scent on the nose and was nicely dry. This wine spent time in French oak barrels, which doesn't have the same harsh, oaky taste of American barrels. Dry and nicely acidic, we found the King's chard to be a pleasant and drinkable wine. We'd chill a bottle or two for a summer cookout to serve with grilled fish.

The '02 cabernet sauvignon, on the other hand, was a little over-oaked after 15 months in the barrels. Still, this wine has nice structure and a pleasing, chocolately finish. Open it up and let it breath for half an hour to let the cherry and coffee flavors build.

David Frost Estate

Frostie brought out his first production in 1997, but the South African's family has actually been producing fine wines for more than 60 years. His grapes are grown in the Paarl region of South Africa, noted for its dry whites, but with some excellent red varietals in the higher elevations.

Frost has always been a good marketer—he sells some of his wines in commemorative bottles featuring colorful labels painted by sports artist LeRoy Neiman. We'll leave it to you to decide if a bottle of shiraz priced normally at about $20 is worth $55 with one of LeRoy's impressionistic paintings on the label!

We tried a bottle of his 2002 Par Excellance Meritage, half cab sauvignon and half cab franc. It opened very fruity, but the finish was slow and lingering with nice tannins and just a hint of minerals. This would accompany a nice grilled steak as nicely as three pars on Amen Corner.

The 2002 Merlot is another nice wine. It opens with tones of plums and dark chocolate, but finishes with a nice oaky twang (the wine spends 18 months in French oak barrels). A very drinkable wine for around $20.

Mike Weir Estates

Yes, Virginia, they grow grapes in Canada—in fact, where in the world don't they make wine these days? 2003 Masters champ and Canada's favorite son grows his grapes in the Niagara region of Ontario, working with Creekside Estates, and the left-hander occasionally blends certain vintages himself.

Like the 2005 Cabernet Shiraz, which opens with notes of currants and strawberries, and then mellows into an oaky spice finish with cloves and pepper. This one's a tap-in for a good red meat dinner.

The 2006 Pinot Grigio is like drinking a fruit salad—it's got aromas of melons and bananas and citrus and berries and peaches and who knows what else. Made us think of sitting on a summer porch, snacking on cheeses and salamis and thinking "life is good."

Finally, don't miss the Vidal Icewine, a specialty of Canada's vintners. The grapes are left on the vines until after the first frost, and that cold snap intensifies the sugars, resulting in a sweet, lovely after-dinner drink. There are lovely tart notes in the '06 bottle we tasted, over a base of honey and flowers.

Players Cellars

Not to be outdone by the rank and file, the PGA Tour just last year entered into a deal with Bermuda Triangle Ventures to create a private-label vintage. With winemaker Brian Zealear, formerly of Napa's Rocking Horse winery, on board, you can look for these wines in stores and at country clubs. And if you can't order it at one of the PGA Tour-owned TPC clubs around the country, well, they ought to fire the marketing manager.

Ever mindful of branding, the Players Cellars label includes a 2003 Sonoma Merlot ($18), a 2004 Santa Barbara Chardonnay ($15) and a 25th anniversary California sparkling wine ($18). Trying to jazz up the Champions (nee Senior) Tour will be a 2003 Monterey Santa Lucia Highlands Syrah ($24), a 2002 Sonoma County Dry Creek Valley Zinfandel ($24), a 2004 Dry Creek Valley Sauvignon Blanc ($18) and a 2003 Monterey Carmel Valley Cabernet Sauvignon ($30). And finally, there's the Commissioner's Private Reserve, no doubt personally chosen by Tim Finchem himself, with such pricy bottles as a 2002 Napa Cabernet Sauvignon from the Rutherford Bench and Stag's Leap District ($60); a 2003 Sonoma Cabernet

Sauvignon sourced from three different vineyards ($44); a 2004 Sonoma Chardonnay from Dry Creek and Carneros ($38); and a 2003 Monterey Santa Lucia Highlands Pinot Noir ($55).

Time, alas, did not allow us to taste them all. But we did find the 2002 cabernet sauvignon from the Private Reserve to have excellent breeding. It opened up with aromas of plums and chocolate, maintained a good mouth feel and ended with a long slow transfiguration on the tongue into notes of cinnamon and licorice. Excellent for toasting a course record or celebrating a hole-in-one.

The Players Cellar Merlot from 2002 was very good in our tasting. It opened with some dark and stormy notes of buttered rum, dark chocolate and berries and finished with some spicy accents at the end. We served it with lasagna and it held its own against the food with good balance. Goes down as easy as a birdie on a short par five.

Obviously, using a professional athlete is something of a marketing gimmick for these wineries. However, we're glad to report that there is actually some good wine in these golfers' bottles. Golf fans will understand if we rank them under par—in golf, that's a good thing.

Breakfast

You can't play good golf on an empty stomach--
even Ben Hogan knew that! To get a golfing day
off to a good start, any one of the following recipes
for eggs, pancakes, waffles or other morning treats is
just the ticket.

Florida Crabmeat Omelet
With Floridian Butter

Another Broken Egg Cafe
Sandestin Golf & Beach Resort
Sandestin, Florida

Ron & Sharon Green, Owners

Serves 2

Ingredients:

For the Floridian Butter

2 cups (4 sticks) butter, softened

½ cup white wine, such as chardonnay or pinot blanc

4 ounces fresh parsley, stems removed, finely chopped

2 ounces garlic powder

For the Crabmeat Omelette

½ cup Floridian Butter

2 ounces cream cheese, cut into strips

3 ounces lump crab meat, shells removed and flaked

½ cup (2 ounces) shredded Monterey Jack cheese

3 eggs, well beaten

To prepare:

For the butter:

Beat the butter in a mixing bowl for 8 minutes or until fluffy. Add the parsley, wine and garlic powder and mix at low speed until well blended. Refrigerate, covered, until ready to use.

For the omelette:

Melt the Floridian Butter in a small saucepan over low heat. Add the crabmeat and cook for

1 minute, stirring occasionally. Set aside. Butter or spray an omelette pan with nonstick cooking spray. Heat the pan over medium heat. Pour in the eggs.

Arrange the cream cheese strips over the eggs just as the eggs begin to set. Flip the omelette upside down and count to 15. Flip the omelette back to the original position. This process will melt the cream cheese into the omelette.

Fold the omelette in half and slide onto an oven-proof ceramic serving plate. Pour the crabmeat mixture over the omelette and sprinkle with the Monterrey Jack cheese.

Place in a warm oven and heat until the cheese melts. Serve with an English muffin and hash brown potatoes. Garnish with fruit.

Gingerbread Waffles

Gasparilla Inn & Club
Boca Grande, Florida

James Dyer, Executive Chef
Yield: about 18 waffles

Ingredients:

18 eggs, beaten until light and fluffy
1 ½ cups sugar
3 cups molasses
6 cups buttermilk
8 ½ cups pastry flour
½ cup cornstarch
2 Tbls ginger
1 Tbls cinnamon
2 tsp cloves, ground
3 tsp salt
1 Tbls baking soda
1 Tbls baking powder
2 ¼ cups (4 1/2 sticks) butter, melted

To prepare:

Beat sugar, molasses and buttermilk into the beaten eggs.

Sift together the flour, ginger, cinnamon, cloves, salt, baking soda and baking powder. Beat the wet ingredients into the dry ingredients.

Stir in butter.

Cook on a hot waffle iron until done. Serve with orange curd and brown sugar syrup.

King & Prince Oatmeal Raisin Muffins

King and Prince Beach & Golf Resort
St. Simons Island, Georgia

Chef Robert Taylor and Chef Robyn Gomez
Yield: 1 dozen

Ingredients:

1 ¼ cups rolled oats
1 ¼ cups buttermilk
2 eggs
¾ cup brown sugar
4 oz. (1 stick) butter; melted and cooled
1 cup flour
1 ¼ tsp baking soda
½ cup raisins

To prepare:

Combine the rolled oats and buttermilk in mixing bowl and let stand for 1 hour.

Add the eggs, brown sugar, and melted butter. Mix for 30 seconds. Scrape down bowl.

Add combined dry ingredients and raisins, mix (low speed) for about 15 seconds or until dry ingredients are moistened.

Fill lightly greased muffin tins ½ full.

Bake, in preheated oven, at 400 degrees for 15-20 minutes.

Oatmeal Pancakes

Gasparilla Inn & Club
Boca Grande, Florida

James Dyer, Executive Chef
Yield: 2 dozen

Ingredients:

4 cups oatmeal
1 cup flour
¼ cup sugar
2 tsp baking soda
2 tsp baking powder
1 tsp salt
4 cups buttermilk
4 eggs, beaten
½ cup (1 stick) butter, melted
3 tsp vanilla
2 bananas, diced
½ cup pecan pieces, toasted

To prepare:

Combine dry ingredients. Add remaining ingredients. Let stand 30 minutes or overnight to thicken. Bake on a heated greased griddle like any other pancake.

Serve with maple syrup and garnish with citrus slices or fresh fruit.

Pinehurst Muffins

Pinehurst Resort
Pinehurst, North Carolina

Scott Rowe, Executive Chef
Yield: 2 dozen

Ingredients:

1 cup carrots, grated
1 cup apples, grated
¼ cup raisins
¼ cup coconut flakes, sweetened
2 eggs
4 ounces oil
1/8 tsp vanilla
¾ cup cake flour
½ cup sugar
¾ tsp baking soda
¾ tsp cinnamon, ground
1/8 tsp salt
1/8 cup pecan pieces

To prepare:

Mix all ingredients by hand in a large bowl.

Pour batter in pre-greased muffin pan, approx. ¾ full.

Bake in preheated 350° oven for 15-20 minutes.

Poached Egg and Black Bean "Brunch" Stack

Forsyth Country Club
Winston-Salem, North Carolina

Michael Mort, Executive Chef
Serves 4

Ingredients:

12 6-inch red or yellow corn tortillas, lightly fried in 2 Tbsp hot oil until crispy
4 black bean cakes (see below)
1 cup cheddar and jack cheeses, shredded
1 cup Romaine lettuce, shredded
½ cup fresh tomatoes, diced
¼ cup green onions, finely minced
1 cup tomato-basil relish (see below)
½ cup sour cream
4 large eggs, soft-poached

For the black bean cakes:
1 cup dry black beans, washed, picked and soaked for 12 hours in refrigerator
¼ cup onions, small diced
¼ cup green bell peppers, small diced
1 Tbls fresh basil, finely chopped
½ Tbls Jalapeno pepper, finely chopped
1 tsp garlic, minced
½ tsp ground black pepper
¼ cup white bread crumbs
Salt to taste
Flour as needed
Olive oil as needed

For the tomato-basil relish:
1 large ripe tomato
1 Tbls chopped basil
1 garlic clove, peeled and finely chopped
2 Tbls red wine vinegar
1 tsp Dijon mustard
4 Tbls virgin olive oil

To prepare:

Tomato-Basil relish:

Cut tomato in half and squeeze out the seeds. Dice flesh into small cubes and set aside. In a medium bowl combine mustard, vinegar and garlic. Whisk in oil. Add tomatoes and basil, stir gently and season to taste with salt and pepper.

Black Bean cakes:

Drain beans, rinse and simmer until tender. Drain and cool. Place in a mixing bowl, add remaining ingredients. With hands, crush beans into lumpy paste, thoroughly combining all ingredients.

Form mixture into eight cakes, about one-inch thick. Lightly coat both sides of cakes with flour and sauté in 2 Tbsp hot oil until golden brown. Serve immediately.

To serve:

Sprinkle some shredded lettuce on 4 dinner plates. Top with crispy tortilla and add a bean cake to each tortilla, topping with shredded cheeses. Top each serving with a second tortilla, add more shredded romaine and diced tomatoes.

Top each with a third tortilla and gently place a poached egg on top. Add a dollop of sour cream on one side of the egg and the fresh tomato-basil relish on the other side. Sprinkle green onions over the top.

Scotch Eggs
With Tabasco Mayonnaise

The Golf Club at Briar's Creek
John's Island, South Carolina

David Tolerton, Executive Chef
Serves 8

Ingredients:

For the eggs:

1 lb ground breakfast sausage meat
Dash of Worcestershire sauce
1 tsp chopped garlic
2 tbsp fresh chopped
    parsley
1 small peeled diced
    onion sautéd & cooled
¼ cup fresh bread
    crumbs
Salt & pepper to season
8 hard boiled eggs
    (peeled & dried with
    a towel to remove any
    excess water.)

For the Tabasco Mayo:

1 cup heavy mayonnaise
Dash each of Worchest-
    er sauce, fresh lemon
    juice & as much
    Tabasco as you
    like or can handle!!
1 tsp chopped fresh garlic
1 tbsp fresh chopped parmessan
Salt & pepper to taste.

To prepare:

For the eggs:
Combine all of the above ingredients (except eggs) in a mixer, using the paddle attachment,

at slow speed until they are well incorporated. Using the palm of your hand, line it with 1oz of the sausage mixture, place the hard boiled egg into the middle of the mix and cover with 1oz more of the sausage mix, and gently roll between both hands until the sausage mix forms a ball with the hard boiled egg in side.

Repeat this process until all eggs are covered. Cook the sausage wrapped eggs in a pre-heated 350F oven, on a greased proof pan for 20-30 minutes, or until sausage is cooked.

Let cool for 3-4 minutes before serving, cut into quarters, serve on mixed field green salad with Tabasco mayo for dipping.

For the Tabasco Mayo:
Combine ingredients and refrigerate for at least 30 minutes before serving. Makes one cup.

29

Southern-Style Eggs Benedict
With Fried Green Tomatoes, Smithfield Ham and Tasso Hollandaise

The Verandah Grill at The Partridge Inn
Augusta, Georgia

Ingredients:

Bradley Czajka, Executive Chef
Serves 2

For the Fried Green Tomatoes:
2 green tomatoes, sliced ¼-inch thick
1 lb cornmeal
1 pint buttermilk
2 tablespoons Tabasco sauce

For the Tasso Hollandaise:
3 egg yolks
2 ounces water
1 tsp rice wine vinegar
10.5 ounces (2 1/2 sticks)
   clarified butter
1 Tbls Tasso ham,
   diced (see Glossary)
4 slices cured ham
4 poached eggs

To prepare:

For the Fried Green Tomatoes:
Add the hot sauce into the buttermilk and season with fresh cracked black pepper. Coat the tomatoes in the buttermilk and let the excess drip off, then crust them with the corn meal. Reserve on a sheet pan with parchment paper.

For the Tasso Hollandaise:
Over a water bath, whisk the egg yolks, water,

and vinegar together until double in volume. Remove from heat and place on a wet towel to keep bowl in place.

Slowly drizzle in the butter to incorporate.

Add the Tasso Ham and a splash of Tabasco.

Fry two tomato slices until they are golden brown.

Poach 4 eggs in a water bath until just soft and towel off the excess liquid.

Place two slices of the cured ham on the fried green tomatoes and top with the poached eggs. Drizzle the hollandaise over the top of the eggs and garnish with a sprig of parsley.

Serve with hash-brown potatoes and roasted tomato.

30

Strata Florentine

Arnold Palmer's Bay Hill Club & Lodge
Orlando, Florida
Robert Lee, Executive Chef
Serves 4

Ingredients:

2 eggs
½ cup milk
½ cup cream
6 ounces chopped spinach
6 ounces chopped prosciutto
1 loaf French bread
¾ cup diced tomatoes
1 cup grated Swiss cheese

To prepare:

Slice French bread and cover the bottom of a 2-quart casserole dish. Layer the spinach, tomato, cheese and prosciutto alternately until ¾" from the top of the dish.

Combine eggs, milk and cream. Pour over the layers and bake at 375 degrees for 45 minutes.

Sweet Potato Scones

Jasmine Porch Restaurant at the Kiawah Island Resort
Kiawah Island, South Carolina

Robert Wysong, Executive Chef
Yield: 20 scones

Ingredients:

5 cups all purpose flour
¾ cup brown sugar
2 Tbls baking powder
1 ½ tsps cinnamon
1 tsp salt
1 tsp ginger
½ tsp allspice
½ lb (2 sticks) butter, cold
2 cups mashed sweet potato (4 potatoes)
1 cup heavy cream
½ cups toasted pecans or walnuts
  (optional)

To prepare:

Combine all dry ingredients.

Cut in the butter with a pastry blender or two knives until the butter is pea-sized.

Combine cream and mashed sweet potatoes.

Mix the wet and dry ingredients together just until a dough forms.

Cut into rounds about 2 inches in diameter and place on cookie sheet lined with parchment paper. Bake at 400° 12-15 min.

32

Tee Time Banana Bread

Long Cove Club
Hilton Head Island, South Carolina

Ingredients:

1 cup sugar
½ cup (1 stick) unsalted butter
2 ripe (or very ripe) bananas
2 large eggs
1 tsp vanilla extract
½ cup chopped walnuts
¼ cup graham cracker crumbs
1 tsp ground cinnamon
1 tsp Kosher salt
1 tsp baking soda
1 cup all-purpose flour

Leonard Giarratano, Executive Chef
Yield: 1 loaf

To prepare:

Cream together the sugar and butter with the paddle attachment of a stand mixer. Add the bananas and eggs. Then add all other dry ingredients and mix.

Grease and paper loaf pan and pour in the batter.

Bake at 350° for one hour and 20 minutes in a conventional oven.

Appetizers

Just in from the course, golfers need something to munch on! In this chapter, our chefs have utilized the South's native treats: shrimp, oysters, sweet potatoes and Vidalia onions to create tasty treats for apres-golf, snacks to serve while watching tournaments on the tube, or to exercise the taste buds before dinner.

Ahi Poke

Steelwood Country Club
Loxley, Alabama
Kevin Peters, Executive Chef
Serves 2

Ingredients:

(Most of these items may be purchased at local Asian markets or in grocery stores with a specialty area)

1 cup sushi rice
2 tablespoons rice wine vinegar
½ tsp sugar
1 ounce avocado diced small ¼ inch pieces
1 ounce golden pine-apple diced small ¼ inch pieces
2 ounces #1 Grade sushi tuna
1 ounce soy sauce
½ ounce sweet soy sauce
½ tsp fresh minced ginger
1 tsp scallion sliced on bias
2 ounces dark sesame oil
1 forming ring 4"diameter and 6" tall
Chile oil to taste

To prepare:

Rinse sushi rice under cold water and drain.

Cook one part rice to two parts water on stove or rice cooker. When finished let cool and fluff with a fork in a wooden bowl. Dissolve sugar in vinegar and pour over rice to season.

Mix the soy, sweet soy, ginger, scallion and sesame oil together in a mixing bowl. In separate bowl add 1 tablespoon soy ginger sauce to tuna and toss.

Place forming ring on the serving plate and spoon rice into the ring, pressing flat with a spoon. Add pineapple and press. Add avocado and press lightly. Finally, add the marinated tuna and press.

Slowly remove the forming ring. Drizzle the remaining soy ginger sauce around the plate and dot with chile oil.

Alabama Crab Cakes
With Fried Green Tomatoes, Crayfish Garnish and Creole Aioli

Grand Hotel Marriott
Point Clear, Alabama

Mike Wallace, Executive Chef

Serves 10

Ingredients:

For the crab cakes:
2 pounds fresh lump crabmeat, picked for shells
½ cup trio peppers, small diced
1/3 cup red onions, small diced
2 Tbls lemon zest or lemongrass
¼ cup garlic chives
¾ cup mayonnaise
1 tsp cayenne pepper
2 Tbls Cajun seasoning
1 Tbls Old Bay seasoning
¼ cup lemon juice
2 whole eggs
2 cups Panko bread crumbs

For the fried tomatoes:
Green tomatoes, sliced in thirds (two slices per plate)
3 ounces flour
3 ounces egg wash
3 ounces cornmeal
Salt and Pepper to taste

For the Creole Aioli:
½ cup Creole mustard
1 tsp minced garlic
1 tsp shallots
1 tsp lemon juice
1 Tbls rice vinegar
1 Tbls honey
½ cup mayonnaise
Salt and Pepper to taste

For a garnish:
10 whole crayfish, steamed
1 cup peppers, brunoise and sauteed
Basil oil
Tomato oil

To prepare:

For the crab cakes:
Place all ingredients except panko bread crumbs in a bowl and mix well. Add panko. Form into 2 ½ inch round cakes and brown on both sides on a griddle or sauté pan. Finish in 350° oven for 3-5 minutes or until done.

For the tomatoes:
Crust two slices by dipping into flour, eggs, and then cornmeal. Deep fry at 350° for 2-3 minutes or saute in hot oil in a frying pan until golden brown.

For the Aioli:
Place all ingredients into a blender and puree until smooth.

To serve:
Drizzle 1 ounce of aioli in a spiral pattern on the plate. Stack tomatoes and crab cakes like a tower. Sprinkle with 1 teaspoon of diced trio peppers and add 1 crayfish to garnish.

Baja Shrimp

Bluewater Bay Resort
Niceville, Florida

Timothy Yeabower, Executive Chef
Serves 4

Ingredients:

**1 pound 40-50 count shrimp, cleaned,
    deveined, tails removed.**
1 cup flour
1 cup ranch salad dressing
1/3 can chipotle peppers, pureed
1 head iceberg lettuce, chopped
1 red pepper, fine dice
1 green onion, sliced

To prepare:

Mix the peppers with the ranch dressing &
place in a large bowl, do not chill.
Dredge the shrimp in the flour & deep fry
or pan saute in hot oil until golden, about 1
minute.

Toss the shrimp with the chipotle dressing &
coat evenly.

Place the lettuce in 4 bowls & place the
shrimp on top.

Garnish with the peppers & onions.

Beef Carpaccio & Baby Arugula Salad With Chervil & Capers Vinaigrette, Bleu Cheese and Pears Croquette

The Ritz-Carlton Golf Resort at Tiburon
Naples, Florida

Derin A. Moore, Executive Chef

Serves 4

Ingredients:

For the Beef Carpaccio:
6 ounces beef tenderloin
2 Tbls mixed grilling seasoning
Salt and pepper to taste

For the Vinaigrette
1 bunch chervil (leaves only)
2 Tbls caper berries (rinsed and drained)
1 shallot (peeled and finely chopped)
1 Tbls red wine vinegar
2 Tbls extra virgin olive oil
2 hard-boiled eggs, coarsely chopped
Sea salt and pepper to taste

For the Baby Arugula Salad:
4 ounces baby arugula (picked)
4 ounces micro greens
1 tsp aged balsamic
1 Tbls extra virgin olive oil

For the Bleu Cheese and Pears Croquette:
4 ounces beef
3 Tbls soya sauce
2 Tbls Mirin (sweet rice wine)
4 ounces bleu cheese
2 Bosc pears
1 cup red wine
½ cup Madeira wine

3 Tbls sugar
2 Tbls Champagne vinegar
2 Star anis
1 cinnamon stick
4 cardamom
1 vanilla bean
½ tsp lemon zest
½ tsp orange zest
Panko breadcrumbs, as needed
All-purpose flour, as needed
Egg wash, as needed

To Prepare:

For the Viniagrette:
Mix all ingredients together in a bowl and whisk.

For the Beef Carpaccio:
Season the Beef Tenderloin and sear it in a hot sauté pan (do not cook the beef).

To hold the round shape of the seared tenderloin, roll it tightly in cling wrap.

Place the beef in the freezer for approximately 30 minutes in order to easily slice it thinly.

For the Baby Arugula Salad:
Mix both Baby Arugula and Micro Greens together with the Balsamic and Oil.

For the Bleu Cheese and Pears Croquette
Marinate one 6 oz piece (1 inch diameter long) Beef Sirloin in Soya Sauce and Mirin for a ½ hour.

Poach the pear and the rest of the ingredients in a pot with wine (except the breadcrumb, flour, egg wash and bleu cheese) until tender: remove from wine and drain.

Cut the beef, cheese and pear into ¼ inch slices using a 1 inch diameter circular cutter. Alternately layer 16 pieces of beef, 12 pieces of pear and 12 pieces of cheese, repeating the layers three times and ending with a beef layer.

Keep stacks together with a skewer through each end. Coat with flour, egg wash and then breadcrumbs.

Deep-fry or pan saute croquettes in hot oil until golden brown.

To serve:
Layer the sliced beef carpaccio on a round plate and drizzle the vinaigrette on the beef with the hard boiled egg.

Mound the arugula salad on top of the beef carpaccio.

Position several of the croquettes around the plate and serve.

39

Baked Oysters Pinehurst

The Pinehurst Resort
Pinehurst, North Carolina
Scott Rowe, Executive Chef
Serves 6

Ingredients:

30 oysters, fresh, shucked
1 Tbls butter
¼ pound country ham, fine julienne
¼ pound spinach leaves, fresh, stems
  removed
½ Tbls garlic, minced
½ Tbls shallots, minced
1 Tbls onion, minced

To prepare:

Warm butter in small sauté pan, add garlic, shallots and onion and cook until translucent. Add spinach, country ham and cook until spinach has a tender texture. Season to taste and reserve.

Place about ½ tablespoon of garnish in each oyster. Coat each oyster with the caviar hollandaise and finish under broiler.

Serve on heated rock salt. Garnish with lemon wedges and parsley.

Carolina Crab Dip

Benvenue Country Club
Rocky Mount, North Carolina

David Baudier, Executive Chef

Ingredients:

3 pounds lump crab meat
½ can artichokes, drained and rinsed
1 pint heavy cream
4 ounces yellow onions, brunoise
2 ounces white wine
2 ounces chopped garlic
12 ounces spinach
12 ounces cream cheese
4 ounces grated Parmesan
Salt and pepper to taste

To prepare:

Sauté onions and garlic in clarified butter, deglaze with white wine.

In a mixing bowl combine cream cheese, onion mixture and heavy cream. Add spinach and artichoke hearts, blend well. Add Parmesan cheese, salt and pepper.

Mix in crabmeat by hand

Pour into a gravy boat or serving dish and wrap with plastic wrap. Refrigerate until ready to serve with crackers or chips.

41

Cajun Bogey Bites

Hollywood Casino Bay St. Louis
Bay St. Louis, Mississippi

Chef Josh, Executive Chef
Yield: about 30

Ingredients:

18 ounces jalapeno peppers, julienne
18 ounces onion, julienne

Egg Wash:
3 whole eggs

1 ½ cups milk
1 tsp salt
1 tsp black pepper

Flour Mix:
3 cups all-purpose flour
2 tsp salt
1 tsp black pepper
1 tsp granulated garlic
1 tsp cayenne pepper
12 ounces raspberry pepper jam (we use
    Anchor brand)

To prepare:

Beat eggs in medium-size mixing bowl, then add milk, salt and pepper and blend well. Set aside.

In separate bowl, mix flour, salt, pepper and garlic.

Preheat hot-oil fryer to 350°. Or pan saute in 1/2 inch of hot oil.

Dredge jalapenos and onions in flour mixture to evenly coat, then dip into egg mixture and evenly coat again. Dredge again in the flour and shake off the excess flour. Fry for approximately 3-5 minutes or until golden brown.

Serve with raspberry pepper jam or similar product.

Chicken Puffs

Harmony Golf Preserve
Harmony, Florida

Kelvin Fitzpatrick, Executive Chef
Yield: About 50 puffs

Ingredients:

3 ounces vegetable oil
1 Tbls salt
1 Tbls black pepper
1 Tbls paprika
1 Tbls minced garlic
10 – boneless, skinless chicken tenders
2 eggs
6 ounces sun-dried tomatoes, julienne in 1" strips
Puff pastry cut into 2" squares
12 ounces Boursin cheese

To prepare:

Combine vegetable oil, garlic and spices for the marinade. Cut chicken tenders into 1-inch cubes and marinate for 4 hours or overnight.

Spread chicken onto baking sheet and partially cook in a 350° oven for about 6 minutes. Remove from oven and cool completely.

Whisk eggs together with 1 ounce water to make an egg wash.

Place half a tablespoon of boursin cheese onto each 2x2 puff pastry square. Top with one piece of sun-dried tomato and one piece of chicken. Fold each corner of the pastry sheet to the center of the filling and close creases tightly.

Spray a baking sheet with cooking spray and place chicken puffs two inches apart, seam side down. Lightly brush each puff with egg wash and bake for 15 minutes in the oven or until golden brown and chicken is fully cooked.

Serve warm with your favorite dipping sauce. The puffs can be prepared up to two days in advance.

43

Coconut Shrimp
with Spicy Citrus Dipping Sauce

Arnold Palmer's Bay Hill Club and Lodge
Orlando, Florida

Robert Lee, Executive Chef
Serves 4

Ingredients:

20 extra-large shrimp, peeled and deveined
1 cup Coco Lopez (cream of coconut)
1 egg, beaten
1 cup Panko Japanese breadcrumbs
1 cup shredded coconut, sweetened

For the dipping sauce:
¾ cup orange marmalade
3 Tbls horseradish
¼ cup orange juice

To prepare:

Mix Coco Lopez and egg together.

Mix breadcrumbs and coconut together.

Dredge the shrimp in flour then dip in egg mixture, then coat with breadcrumb mixture.

Deep fry or pan saute in hot oil until golden brown. Serve with dipping sauce made by combining the orange marmalade, horseradish and orange juice.

Country Ham Pate-A-Choux

Pine Lake Country Club
Charlotte, North Carolina

Ken Snyder, Executive Chef
Serves 6

Ingredients:

For the filling:
¼ pound country ham
8 ounces cream cheese
1 Tbls Dijon mustard
1 tsp regular mustard
1 Tbls mayonnaise
½ tsp black pepper

For the Pate A Choux dough:
¼ pound (1 stick)butter
'1 cup all-purpose flour
1 cup hot water
4 eggs
¼ tsp salt

To prepare:

For the dough:
In small sauce pot add water, butter, salt on medium high heat. When butter is melted add flour. Reduce heat to low and stir vigorously with a wooden spoon for 5-8 minutes or until the flour is cooked out. Do not allow to brown.

Transfer dough to a stand mixer with paddle attachment. Add 1 egg at a time at medium speed, mixing well. Fill pastry bag with dough. Using a round tip, make quarter-size circles about ½ inch high on a baking sheet pan with parchment paper.

Bake in a 400° preheated oven, for about 10 minutes or until lightly browned. Let cool before filling.

For the filling:
Place the ham in a food processor and chop until fine. Add softened cream cheese, both mustards, mayonnaise and pepper and mix. Mixture should be soft like cake icing.

Using a pastry bag, fill pate-a-choux using a small round tip or cut off edge of top and fill. Unfilled pate a choux can be kept in a plastic bag for a week or frozen for a month.

Serve on a platter as finger-food.

Crab, Spinach & Artichoke Dip
With Pita Chips

Rock Hill Country Club
Rock Hill, South Carolina
Jan K. Leithe, Chef

Yield: 1 9-inch casserole

Ingredients:

For the dip:
1 cup cream cheese
2 Tbls mayonnaise
2 cups fresh spinach, chopped
1 cup quartered canned artichoke hearts
1 can lump crabmeat
1 Tbls chopped basil
1 tsp chopped garlic
2 Tbls chopped scallions
½ tsp salt
½ tsp pepper
1 cup grated Parmesan cheese

For the chips:
4 pita bread slices, cut into triangles
2 Tbls Old Bay seasoning
¼ cup oil

To prepare:

For the dip:
Place all ingredients (except half the Parmesan cheese) into a mixer and combine until well incorporated. Do not overmix.

Remove and place in a nine-inch casserole dish. Sprinkle remaining cheese on top and bake in a 325° oven for about 20 minutes.

For the chips:
Mix the pita triangles, oil and seasoning together. Place on a baking sheet and place in a 325° oven for 10-15 minutes. Make sure chips are crispy.

46

Crawfish Beignuts

Musgrove Country Club
Jasper, Alabama
Phil Schirle, Executive Chef
Yield: about 20

Ingredients:

6 whole eggs
12 ounces beer
1/2 cup hot sauce
1/2 cup Cajun Power Garlic Sauce
1/2 Tbls salt
2 Tbls Creole seasoning
5 tsp baking powder
4 Tbls roasted garlic puree
1 1/2 cups green onions, small chopped
1 red bell pepper, small diced
4 3/4 cups cake flour
1 pound crawfish tail meat with fat

To prepare:

Mix all ingredients. Scoop to the size of a quarter and fry in 300° oil until golden brown and cooked throughout.

Serve with Jalapeno tartar sauce or Jalapeno relish or your favorite dipping sauce.

Fennel & Black Pepper Goat Cheese
on Toast Points

Daniel Island Club
Charleston, South Carolina
Tyler Dudley, Executive Chef
Serves 6-8

Ingredients:

16 ounces soft goat cheese
3 Tbls chopped fresh tarragon
2 Tbls fennel seeds, finely crushed
4 tsp lemon zest
1 tsp cracked black pepper

To prepare:

Place goat cheese, chopped tarragon, fennel seeds, lemon zest, and pepper in mixer.

Mix on low speed until all ingredients are incorporated.

Spread mixture on freshly toasted baguette toast points, or with crackers or pita chips.

Fried Oysters
With Buttermilk Dressing
New Bern Golf & Country Club
New Bern, North Carolina

Gabriel Maldonado, Executive Chef
Serves 4

Ingredients:

For the dressing:
1 Tbls fresh chopped dill
1 Tbls fresh chopped tarragon
1 cup buttermilk or plain yogurt
¼ cup white wine vinegar
2 Tbls finely diced shallot
   shallots
1 Tbls of sugar
Pinch salt
Pinch pepper

For the fried oysters:
½ cup all purpose flour
20 shucked medium size
   oysters
3 whole eggs
2 Tbls water
1 cup of Japanese Panko breadcrumbs
1 Tbls of ground curry
Pinch salt
Pinch pepper
Oil for frying

For the garnish:
1 head of Bibb lettuce wash and dried
1 cup of diced roma tomatoes
10 caper berries or ¼ cup of capers
   (optional)

To prepare:

For the dressing:
In a bowl combine all the ingredients and set aside.

For the fried oysters:
Combine the curry, salt and pepper with flour and set aside.

Mix the eggs with the water to make an egg wash set aside.

Dredge the oyster in the flour and shake to remove excess flour. Dip the oysters into the egg wash, strain, transfer to breadcrumbs to coat them thoroughly and place in a sheet pan (don't stack them). Refrigerate for 30 minutes.

Add about 1/2 inch of oil to a frying pan and fry the oysters until golden brown and crisp.

Place in a plate with paper towesl to absorb excess oil. Keep warm.

On a dinner plate place the lettuce and 5 oysters drizzle with dressing, tomatoes and caper berries. Serve immediately.

49

Lobster Cheesecake

Pawleys Plantation Golf & Country Club
Pawleys Island, South Carolina

Christopher Spina, Executive Chef
Yield: 12-16

Ingredients:

2 pounds cream cheese, at room temperature
7 eggs
2 cups grated Parmesan cheese
1 cup lobster meat, cooked
¼ cup red bell pepper, diced fine
¼ cup chives
¼ cup red onion, diced fine

To prepare:

Beat cream cheese and egg in mixer until smooth.

In a large mixing bowl, mix in remaining ingredients and pour into ungreased cupcake liners.

Bake at 300° for 1 hour and check with a toothpick. You want it to come out clean just like when you are baking a cake.

Once the cheesecakes are fully cooked, remove from the oven and let them cool at room temperature.

PHOTO COURTESY OF PAWLEY'S PLANTATION

Lobster Wellington
With Lobster Crab Cream

Hendersonville Country Club
Hendersonville, North Carolina

Steve Greenhoe, Executive Chef
Serves 6

Ingredients:

3 six-ounce lobster tails
4 Tbls (1/2 stick) butter
2 Tbls onion, coarse chopped
2 Tbls carrots, coarse chopped
3 Tbls flour
2 tsp sugar
1 ½ cup water
2 Tbls lobster base
4 ounces heavy cream
3 Tbls sherry
3 ounces lump crab meat
2 cups spinach, blanched, drained and
    chopped
4 Tbls shredded asiago cheese
    (or parmesan)
Bread crumbs
Salt and pepper to taste
6 5-inch puff pastry squares

To prepare:

Remove lobster meat from shells reserving shells. Split the tails down the center and rinse in cold water, taking care to remove any bits of shell.

Skewer the lobster tails from end to end with wooden skewers. Poach in lightly salted water until the glassy appearance is gone. Remove from water and set aside. Do not remove the skewers.

In a small sauce pan sauté the lobster shells, carrots and onions in butter until the vegetables are soft but not browned. The shells will add flavor. Add flour and stir well. Add water, lobster base and sugar and bring to a simmer, stirring well. Reduce heat and add heavy cream and sherry and strain to remove vegetables and shells. Add crab meat and return to low heat. Keep warm.

Combine spinach, asiago cheese and 3 ounces of lobster sauce. Season with salt and pepper and add bread crumbs as needed. Spread spinach stuffing over three-quarters of each pastry square and place one piece of lobster tail, skewer removed, across each of the squares. Dampen the remaining edge of the squares with a little water to help seal and carefully roll the pastry around the stuffing and lobster, making certain that the edge seals.

Place the lobster rolls on a cookie sheet and bake at 400° for 8-10 minutes until the pastry is golden brown. Remove from oven and let rest.
To Plate: Place 2 to 3 tablespoons of the lobster sauce in the middle of each plate. Carefully slice the pastry rolls and arrange slices over the lobster sauce. Garnish with tomato rose and basil leaf.

51

Louisiana Crab Cakes
With Remoulade Sauce

Wexford Plantation
Hilton Head Island, South Carolina
Frank Copeland, Executive Chef

Serves 4

Ingredients:

For the Crab Cakes:
1 pound fresh lump crab meak (picked to remove shells)
½ cup red, yellow and green bell peppers, small diced
1 bunch cilantro, chopped
1 bunch green onions, chopped
1 Tbls grain mustard
2-3 cups white bread crumbs
1-2 cups heavy mayonnaise
Salt and pepper to taste
Tabasco and Worcestershire sauce to taste
Pinch of blackening spice (optional)
2 cups oil for frying

For the Remoulade Sauce:
¼ cup fresh lemon juice
¾ cup prepared mayonnaise
½ cup chopped yellow onions
½ cup chopped green onions
¼ cup chopped celery
2 Tbls prepared horseradish
2 Tbls minced garlic
3 Tbls Creole or whole-grain mustard
3 Tbls ketchup
3 Tbls chopped flat-leaf parsley
1 Tbls kosher salt
¼ tsp cayenne pepper
1/8 tsp fresh ground black pepper

To prepare:

For the Remoulade Sauce:
Put all the ingredients in a food processor and process for 30 seconds. Use immediately or store. Will keep well in airtight container in refrigerator for several weeks.

For the Crab Cakes:
Mix the crab meat, peppers, cilantro, green onion, mustard and mayonnaise in a bowl. Add Tabasco, Worcestershire, salt and pepper to taste. Add bread crumbs in small amounts until the mixture binds together. Shape into cakes 2-3 inches round.

Dredge the cakes in remaining bread crumbs.

Heat oil in large skillet over medium heat. When oil is hot, add the crab cakes and fry for two minutes on each side or until golden brown. Drain on paper towels.

Place on a serving plate while hot and drizzle with the Remoulade sauce. Garnish with fresh greens, chopped parsley or lemon wedge.

Note: these cakes will freeze well. When using from freezer, allow them to defrost thoroughly. Dredge in bread crumbs to soak up any excess water from defrosting.

Lowcountry Oysters Rockefeller
Pawleys Plantation Golf & Country Club
Pawleys Island, South Carolina

Christopher Spina, Executive Chef
Yield: 3 dozen

Ingredients:

½ pound (2 sticks) unsalted butter
1 Tbls fresh parsley, chopped
¼ cup celery, chopped
¼ cup corn kernels
3 ounces apple smoked bacon, diced
½ cup shredded parmesan cheese
¼ cup shallots, chopped
1 tsp garlic, chopped
½ cup fresh spinach, chopped
2 ounces dark rum
¼ cup fresh bread crumbs
Salt and pepper, to taste
36 oysters on the half shell
Rock salt, as needed

To prepare:

Heat the butter in a sauté pan. Add the bacon, parsley, celery, corn, shallots and garlic and cook for 4 to 5 minutes. Add the spinach and cook for 1 minute. Add the cheese, rum and bread crumbs; season with salt and pepper.

Transfer the mixture to a food processor and purée. Top each oyster with approximately 2 teaspoons of the vegetable mixture; it should coat the oyster's entire surface.

Bake the oysters on a bed of rock salt at 450° until the mixture bubbles, approximately 6-7 minutes. Serve hot.

Lychee Glazed Shrimp

Hammock Bay Golf & Country Club
Naples, Florida

Joetta DeFrancesco, Food & Beverage Manager
Desmond Maguire, Chef
Serves 4

Ingredients:

1 Tbls olive oil
1 shallot minced
½ Anaheim Chili- or another hot pepper
2 small cloves garlic
1 20 oz. can lychees in syrup
1 Tbls honey
½ bunch cilantro chopped
1 pound shrimp peeled and deveined
1 package sugar cane skewers (can usually be found in produce section)
Sirachi chili paste

To prepare:

Sautee shallots, chili and garlic in a sauce pan in oil over medium heat until shallots are translucent.

In a food processor puree entire can of lychees and syrup until almost smooth. Add in sautéed shallot mixture and pulse until combined. Return lychee and shallot mixture to the stove then add honey. Simmer until mixture

thickens enough to coat shrimp. Remove mixture from heat and cool. Reserve ¼ of mixture to use as sauce when serving shrimp. Use remaining ¾ of cooled mixture to toss with cleaned shrimp in a medium bowl. Let mixture marinate in refrigerator for 30 minutes.

Skewer shrimp on sugar cane skewers and grill over medium flame until cooked through. Mixture will caramelize on shrimp so be sure to turn skewers at least once to prevent burning.

Remove shrimp from heat and place on plate. Drizzle shrimp skewers with remaining lychee mixture and dot sirachi chili paste around the plate. Sprinkle plates with chopped cilantro and serve.

Shrimp may be served as an entrée on a bed of rice or on a salad with a light citrus vinaigrette.

Mango Shrimp

High Hampton Inn & Country Club
Cashiers, North Carolina

Bob Scholler, Executive Chef
Serves 4

Ingredients:

For the Shrimp:
1 pound 16-18 shrimp, peeled and deveined
2 cups evaporated milk
1 cup all purpose flour
2 Tbls salt
1/2 Tbls white pepper
1 tsp garlic powder

For the Sauce:
16 ounces Major Grey's chutney
1/4 tsp Tabasco sauce
¼ pound (1 stick) butter
4 ounces (1/2 cup) heavy cream

To prepare:
Preheat deep fat fryer to 350°.

Wash shrimp and place in a bowl. Cover with evaporated milk.

Mix seasonings with flour and reserve.

Place sauce ingredients in a heavy bottomed sauce pot and stir together over medium-low heat until well combined.

Lightly dredge shrimp in seasoned flour and fry in oil until golden brown. (Can be sauteed in heavy pan).

Remove from oil and toss in sauce in a mixing bowl.

Serve immediately.

Mississippi Sin

Bear Creek Golf Club
Laurel, Mississippi

Bertha Cooley, Executive Chef

Serves 6-8

Ingredients:

1 ½ cups sour cream
1 8-ounce package, cream cheese
Small bunch green onion, chopped
1 package, sliced ham, cubed
1 small can green chilies, chopped
2 cups cheddar cheese, grated
1 loaf, round Hawaiian bread

To prepare:

Soften cream cheese and greated cheese in the microwave for one minute or until well blended.

Add sour cream, onions, ham and chilies. Mix well.

Scoop out the center of the bread, reserving the top. Fill with cheese mixture, topping with reserved bread top. Cover loaf with aluminum foil and bake in aluminum pan for one hour at 350°. Remove foil and bread top. Serve with crackers or chips for dipping.

Oyster & Spinach Gratin

Rosen Shingle Creek Resort
Orlando, Florida
James R. Slattery, Executive Chef
Serves 8

Ingredients:

½ cup apple-smoked bacon, finely
  julienned
1 cup onion, fine diced
1 cup celery, fine diced
2 Tbls chopped garlic
1 Tbls butter
¼ cup Pernod
Flour
Liquid from 1 pint of oysters
½ gallon milk
2 cups spinach, finely chopped
½ cup Gruyere cheese
½ cup Parmesan cheese
1 Tbls Tabasco sauce

To prepare:

Render the bacon in a large pot until it begins to brown. Melt the butter and sweat the onion, celery and garlic for 5 minutes. Add the Pernod and cook for 5 minutes.

Slowly whisk in flour until all the liquid has been absorbed. Whisk in an addition ¼ cup of flour at that point. Slowly add milk while whisking. Once all the milk has been added, season with salt and white pepper.

Add the spinach, Tabasco, Worcestershire sauce and oyster liquid (if there is no liquid, use pureed oysters). Continue to cook for 15 minutes on low heat, continually whisking to avoid scorching. Taste to make sure the flour has cooked out.

Remove from heat and fold in the cheeses. Taste for seasoning again.

To serve: place in a serving dish and sprinkle grated cheese on top along with the chopped parsley as garnish. Serve with croutons or toast points for dipping.

Rock Shrimp Stuffed Calimari With Fried Baby Artichokes and Spicy Marinara

Addison Reserve Country Club
Delray Beach, Florida

Sean Key, Executive Chef

Serves 6-8

Ingredients:

6 Large U-10 calamari tubes cleaned
5 ½ cups spicy marinara sauce (see below)

For the Stuffing:
2 pounds rock shrimp, cooked and finely chopped
1 medium onion peeled and small diced
1 Tbls olive oil
3 cloves garlic, minced
2 ounces Prosciutto, fine diced
½ cup white wine
1 ½ cups sour dough croutons, small diced
½ cup shrimp stock
4 Tbls parsley, chopped fine
8 basil leaves chiffanade

For the Sauce:
½ medium onion, peeled and small diced
3 cloves garlic, minced
3 Tbls olive oil
5 cups canned tomatoes with juice
½ tsp fresh thyme
1 Tbls fresh oregano
5 large basil leaves chopped
Crushed red pepper to taste

For the Fried Baby Artichokes:
6 baby artichokes, cleaned, cut in half and soaked in acidic water
2 cups seasoned all-purpose flour
Oil for frying

To Prepare:

For the Stuffing:
Sautee prosciutto, onions and garlic in 2 Tbls oil 5-6 minutes until onions are translucent, being careful not to burn. Deglaze with wine and cook until almost dry. Remove from heat. Mix together with rock shrimp, croutons, parsley and basil. Add shrimp stock and fold mixture together, season with salt and pepper and reserve.

For the Sauce:
Saute onion and garlic in 2 Tbls oil until translucent. Add tomatoes and herbs, bring to a simmer, reduce heat to low and simmer 30 minutes. Add crushed pepper to taste, season with salt and remove from heat. Using a blender, pulse the hot sauce in batches until smooth and reserve warm.

For the Fried Baby Artichokes:
Toss artichokes in flour, shake off excess. Deep-fry or saute in oil until tender. Remove and season with salt, reserve warm.

Stuff each calamari tube to the top with stuffing and close open end with a toothpick. Place tubes in a Dutch oven or braising pan, add warm sauce and simmer covered on low heat for one hour. Remove from pan, discard toothpicks. Whisk sauce and ladle on plate, add sliced tubes and garnish with artichokes.

58

Roasted Fennel Souffle

Ginn Reunion Resort
Orlando, Florida

Christian W. Schmidt, Executive Chef
Serves 8 small or 4 large portions

Ingredients:

2 heads of fennel, cut in half
1 tsp salt
1/2 tsp black pepper
2 Tbls heavy cream
1 ounce pecorino cheese, grated
4 large egg yolks, beaten
4 large egg whites, beaten stiff peaks
1/2 cup whole milk
1 Tbls butter
1 Tbls all-purpose flour
Other items:
2 Tbls toasted pine nuts
1 head of frisse lettuce
2 ounces extra virgin olive oil
Snipped chives or micro basil

To prepare:

Preheat oven to 350°. Roast fennel for 45 minutes or until cooked.

Meanwhile, melt butter in a sauce pan on medium heat and add the flour to form a thick paste. Slowly add the milk and cream until the paste becomes thinner and thinner, but not lumpy. A runny sauce should be formed. Season with salt and black pepper and slowly heat until thickened, stirring continuously. Set aside

Once the fennel is done, place in a food processor while still warm and puree with a little olive oil.

In a dry stainless mixing bowl add puree, pecorino cheese and beaten egg yolks and combine.

In a mixer whip the egg whites until a stiff peak has been achieved. Fold the egg whites into the fennel mixture until smooth.

Spray a soufflé container with nonstick cooking spray or butter. Delicately fill each container with fennel mix until just below the lip. Tap them to allow mix to settle and release trapped air. Place evenly spaced containers on sheet tray and place in 350° oven for 20 minutes or until golden on top. Allow souffles to rest for 5 minutes while you arrange your plates.

To plate:
Arrange a little bed of the frisse lettuce. Sprinkle the toasted pine nuts around and drizzle lettuce and plate with extra virgin olive oil
Carefully remove the soufflé from the container and rest upon the frisse. Garnish with some micro opal basil or chive sticks

Seared Scallops
With Fava Bean Risotto & Chive Butter

Ballantyne Resort, Hotel & Spa
Charlotte, North Carolina

Kirk Gilbert, Executive Chef

Serves 4

Ingredients:

For the Scallops:
6-8 U-8 scallops
Salt and pepper to taste

For the Chive Butter:
¼ pound (1 stick) butter
¼ pound chives
Salt and pepper to taste

For the Risotto:
½ small sweet onion
2 cloves garlic
¼ cup white wine
1 cup risotto
¼ cup Parmesan cheese, grated
3 Tbls unsalted butter
2-3 cups low-sodium chicken stock
3-4 tablespoons heavy cream
1 cup blanched Fava beans
Salt and pepper to taste
2 tablespoons olive oil

To prepare:

For the Chive Butter:
Soften butter. Blanch chives in salted water until puree-able but not so much as to cause a loss of color. Puree chives in a blender, then pass through a fine sieve. Combine puree with softened butter, mixing thoroughly. Season to taste. Reserve in refrigerator.

For the Risotto:
Dice onion, mince garlic. In medium sauce pan sweat the onion and garlic in oil until opaque. Add risotto, toast lightly. Deglaze with white wine. Add ½ of the chicken stock, stirring constantly. Continue adding chicken stock as needed until rice is al dente. Add favas. Finish with cream, Parmesan and butter. Season to taste.

For the Scallops:
In large skillet over high heat, add 3-4 table-spoons vegetable oil and carefully place scallops one at a time spread evenly in pan. Brown on both sides, approximately 2-3 min. each side. Remove scallops and reserve on separate plate. Drain excess oil from pan, and add 1 cup cream and the liquid from seared scallops. Reduce cream by half then whisk in the chive butter. Season to taste.

To serve:
On large platter spoon risotto onto plate, arrange scallops around and drizzle with chive butter sauce.

Seared Scallops
With Foie Gras, Port Marinated Figs & GoatCheese

Haig Point Club
Daufuskie Island, South Carolina
Gerard Brunett, Executive Chef

Serves 4

Ingredients:

4 U10 Scallops
4 2-ounce pieces foie gras, at room
 temperature (canned or fresh-made)
2 Black Mission figs, quartered
1 ounce grape seed oil
4 1-ounce "wedges" goat cheese
1 cup fine quality port wine
1/8 cup honey
Fresh thyme leaves
Salt
Pepper

To prepare:

In a small sauce pan, combine the honey &
port and bring to a simmer. Reduce by ¼.
Allow port to cool to room temp and add the
figs. Marinate for at least 3 hours or overnight.

Remove the figs from the marinade and allow
to warm to room temp. Place the marinade
liquid in a sauce pan and warm just to a simmer and remove from heat. Place the goat
cheese wedges on 4 plates. Heat two 10 inch
sauté pans over medium high heat. Add the
grape seed oil to one. Season scallops & foie
gras with salt & pepper. Place scallops in sauté
pan with grape seed oil and the foie gras in
the other. Sear both sides of the foie gras and
scallop, cooking the foie gras to a "medium-
rare" temperature and the scallop to a "medium" temperature. Immediately remove the foie
gras and scallops from the pans.

Place one scallop on each of the plates. Place a
piece of foie gras atop the scallop. Garnish the
plate with the figs and drizzle a small amount
of the fig marinade o each piece of cheese and
the plate.

Finish with thyme leaves.

Spinach & Artichoke Dip

Gray Plantation Golf Club
Lake Charles, Louisiana
Kyle Clawson, Chef
Serves 6-8

Ingredients:

1 pack frozen spinach or fresh if available
1 jar artichoke hearts chopped
2 quarts heavy cream
1 pound cream cheese
1 cup shredded parmesan cheese
3 cloves roasted garlic
3 ounces sun dried tomatoes chopped
Salt and pepper to taste

To prepare:

Sauté spinach until wilted.

Add roasted garlic and sun dried tomatoes, sauté 5 minutes.

Add cream cheese and heavy cream stirring until combined, add artichokes and parmesan cheese to thicken.

Salt and pepper to taste.

Serve with grilled pita bread or tortilla chips.

Taboule Dip

Club Med Sandpiper
Port St. Lucie, Florida

Erik Peters, Chef

Serves 4

Ingredients:

1/2 cup couscous
1/2 cup chicken stock -- boiling
1/2 large onion -- diced small
1/2 whole tomato -- diced small
1/2 whole bell pepper -- diced small
3 1/2 tsp olive oil
3 sprigs basil leaves -- chopped
1 Tbls lemon juice
salt and white pepper -- to taste

To prepare:

Place the dry couscous in a bowl and add half a teaspoon of the olive oil and a pinch of salt. Mix for a minute or so with your fingers to coat all the grains. This will ensure that the grains will not stick together and form clumps.

Shake the container slightly so the grains level out. Pour the hot chicken stock over the couscous and then cover the bowl with plastic wrap and let sit for 5-7 minutes or until the grains have absorbed all the liquid.

While the couscous is absorbing the liquid, cut the vegetables.

Once the couscous has fully absorbed the liquid, fluff lightly with a spoon or fork for a minute or so. Add the other ingredients and mix together. Season with salt and pepper.

Serve with warm nan bread, pita crackers or other bread. Taboule can be stored in refrigertator.

Lunch & Salads

When making the turn, most golfers will settle for a hog dog or a burger. But if there's time, some of these delicious recipes for sandwiches, quick and nourishing lunches or tasty salads will provide better nutrition and make your golfer much, much happier (and healthier!).

Barbecue Pork Sandwiches

Pinehurst Resort
Pinehurst, North Carolina
Scott Rowe, Executive Chef
Yield: About 10 sandwiches

Ingredients:

1 4-5 pound boneless pork butt
1 cup apple cider vinegar
2 tsp crushed red pepper
2 tsp black pepper
Salt to taste
1/4 cup brown sugar

To prepare:

Cut deep slashes in pork butts.

Combine remaining ingredients in lexan container. Mixture should be somewhat salty.

Marinate pork overnight, turning over several times.

Place pork in smoker and smoke at 225° for 2 hours.

Move pork to oven and cook at 300° until very tender.

Remove pork from oven and cool until it can be handled.

Shred pork while still warm with gloved hands.

Refrigerate until ready to use.

Serve on fresh baked rolls with french fries and cole slaw, garnish with a dill pickle.

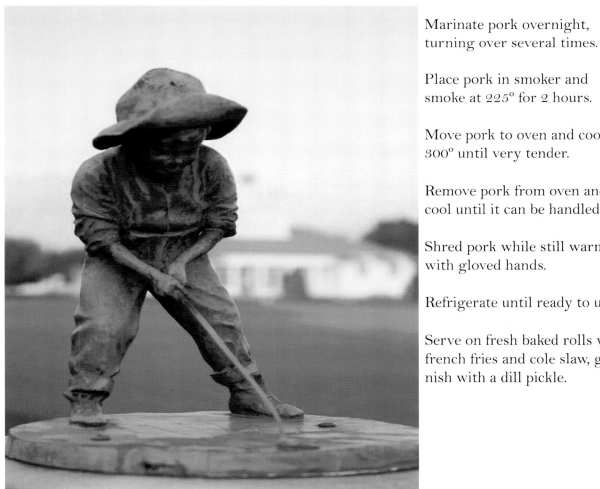

Bleu Cheeseburgers
with Burgundy Demi-Glace & Fried Onions

Oak Grove Island Golf & Country Club
Brunswick, Georgia
Jacqueline Grantham-Watson, Chef
Serves 4

Ingredients:

For the Burgers:
2 pounds ground chuck
4 Kaiser rolls
4 Tbls bleu cheese crumbles
½ tsp each of salt, pepper and garlic
   powder
Lettuce, tomato wedges (optional)

For the Burgundy Demi – Glace:
2 quarts Demi-Glace
½ cup Burgundy wine (one you would
   drink)
1 Tbls beef base
2 tsp cornstarch
Water as needed
Salt and pepper (optional)

For the Onions:
1 large onion (Vidalia of course)
1 cup self- rising flour
½ cup milk
1 tsp each of salt, pepper, garlic powder
   and cayenne pepper
Oil for frying
Paper towels

To prepare:

For the Burgundy Demi – Glace:
In a medium saucepot over medium heat, re-duce wine by two-thirds. Whisk together wine and demi-glace. Turn the heat to low: con-tinue by making slurry with the cornstarch and water. Add this to the sauce and turn heat back up to medium; and cook while stirring to thicken about 2-3 minutes. Taste and season with salt and pepper as needed. Set aside.

For the Onions:
Thinly slice onions; soak in milk. Mix flour and seasonings. In batches dredge onions into flour and fry in oil heated to 325° till brown and crisp; drain on paper towels; set aside.

For the Burgers:
Preheat grill or flattop to 350°. Shape ground chuck into four patties; season.

Cook until at least 160°. Top each patty with one tablespoon of cheese to partially melt. Re-warm demi-glace.

Toast Kaiser rolls on flattop. Place a patty on top of bottom bun; spoon warmed sauce on top: then place a heap of fried onions atop. On top bun place lettuce and tomato wedge then serve with french fries.

Charleston Crab Cakes
With Andouille Succotash & Grain Mustard Sauce

Daniel Island Club
Charleston, South Carolina
Tyler Dudley, Chef
Serves 4

Ingredients:

For the Crab Cakes
3/4 cup mayonnaise
1 egg
1 tsp cayenne
1 tsp old bay
1 tsp dry mustard
2 Tbls fresh lemon juice
6 Tbls Panko Japanese breadcrumbs
2 pounds jumbo lump crab
1 pound slipper lobster* meat, chopped
Flour for dredging
*related to rock lobster, often imported frozen

For the Andouille Succotash:
2 Tbls butter
¼ cup red onion, brunoise
2 cups lima beans, par cooked
2 cups corn kernels, fresh or frozen
1/4 lb andouille sausage, cut in half then
   thin sliced
2 cups tomatoes, brunoise
2 Tbls parsley, chopped
2 tsp fresh lime juice

For the mustard sauce:
½ cup white wine
3 Tbls brandy
1 cups heavy cream
½ cup whole grain mustard
Juice of one lemon
½ teaspoon kosher salt

To prepare:

Crab Cakes:
Whisk mayonnaise and eggs together. Whisk in next five ingredients until incorporated.

Gently fold in crab and lobster.
Divide into 4-ounce cakes, about 3 inches wide. Coat with flour and pan sear in 2-3 Tbls hot oil.

Succotash:
Saute onions in butter until translucent. Add corn and sausage and sauté for 5 minutes and season with salt and pepper. Add cooked beans and tomatoes and heat through. Remove from heat and add parsley and lime juice. Check seasoning.

Sauce:
Reduce wine and brandy to au sec (almost dry). Whisk in cream and reduce heat to medium and simmer till sauce thickens.

Remove from heat and add mustard.
Add juice and salt.
Adjust seasoning.

To serve: Place succotash in middle of plate, top with crab cake and drizzle with mustard sauce.

67

Citrus Salmon Salad

Canongate at Mirror Lake
Villa Rica, Georgia

Joe Langford, F&B Director
Serves 4

Ingredients:

4 4-ounce salmon filets, skin on
6 ounces mixed salad greens with arugula
3 ounces mandarin orange sections, canned
¾ cup whole roasted pecans
¼ cup craisins (dried cranberries)
¼ cup diced roma tomato
¼ cup blue cheese crumbles
½ cup sliced red onion
¼ tsp fresh cracked black pepper
2 ounces balsamic vinaigrette dressing

For the Marinade:
¼ cup orange juice
¼ cup lime juice
¼ cup lemon juice

To prepare:

For the Salmon
Mix together the marinade ingredients and pour over salmon filet. Allow salmon to marinate for 1 hour.

Place salmon skin side down on preheated 350° grill. Allow to cook 4 minutes and turn over for additional 3-4 minutes.

Salmon will be done prior to flaking remove at 140 degrees at thickest part

For the salad:
Preheat oven to 300°. Roast pecans in baking dish for 25 minutes, allow to cool.

In a large mixing bowl toss salad greens, roasted pecans, and craisins.

To serve:
Divide salad greens into portions and add mandarin oranges, blue cheese crumbles and red onion slices.

Drizzle with balsamic vinaigrette dressing.

Top with salmon filet and cracked pepper over salad – three turns.

68

Crab & Avocado Salad
With Shaved Fennel, Sweet Pea Puree and Confit Cherry Tomatoes

San Jose Country Club
Jacksonville, Florida

Jean-Christophe Setin, Executive Chef

Serves 2

Ingredients:

6 ounces of colossal jumbo crab meat

6 ounces green peas

1/2 bulb fresh fennel

1 ripe avocado

1 Meyer lemon

Fresh chives

6 ripe cherry tomatoes

Two handfuls of micro greens.

2 ounces heavy cream

Salt and cracked black pepper

Extra virgin olive oil

To prepare:

The night before, peel the cherry tomatoes by immersing them in boiling salted water for a few seconds and placing them in an ice bath and then peeling them by hand. Place the peeled tomatoes in a container and cover with olive oil. Place the container in a warm oven (250F) overnight covered.

In a pot of salted boiling water, blanch the

peas until tender (add 1 tsp baking soda to the water to retain color).

Drain the peas and place in a blender, puree until smooth with the heavy cream and season with salt and pepper. Set aside at room temperature.

In a stainless steel bowl, mix the crab, the avocado, the shaved (sliced very thin with a chinese mandolin) fennel bulb, a drizzle of olive oil, salt, pepper from the grinder, half of a lemon's juice and the chopped chives.

Mix well being careful not to break the clusters of crab too much.

Wine Suggestion: Cake Bread, Napa Valley.

69

Crab Cakes
On Creamy Succotash & Roasted Pepper Coulis
The Verandah Grill at The Partridge Inn
Augusta, Georgia

Bradley Czajka, Chef
Serves 4

Ingredients:

For the Crab Cakes:
1 pound crabmeat, lump
1 ounce red pepper, brunoise
1 ounce green pepper, brunoise
1 ounce red onion, brunoise
1 tsp garlic, minced
½ cup mayonnaise
2 Tbls Dijon mustard
2 egg yolks, beaten slightly
¼ cup Panko bread crumbs
1 Tbls Old Bay seasoning
Salt and pepper to taste

For the Roasted Pepper Coulis:
4 red peppers, roasted and peeled
2 Tbls shallots, sliced
1 tsp garlic, minced
1 cup chicken stock

For the Succotash:
2 cups sweet corn kernels
2 cups black-eyed peas, cooked with ham
   hock
1 can tomatoes, diced
1 cup okra, sliced
1 Tbls butter
Salt and pepper to taste

To prepare:

For the Crab Cakes:
Sauté the peppers and onions in a little butter
and then cool.

Fold all the ingredients together in a mixing bowl and then portion into 2 ounce balls, about 6-8 in all. Bread in flour, egg wash and bread crumbs and fry to a golden brown.

For the Roasted Pepper Coulis:
In a sauce pan combine all and bring to a simmer. Place into a blender and puree until smooth. Adjust seasonings with salt and pepper and strain through a chinois.

Let cool then place in a squirt bottle.

For the Succotash:
Bring the corn, black-eyed peas and tomatoes to a simmer in a sauce pot and season. Once the consistency comes together add in the okra and let simmer for an additional 3 minutes. Adjust seasonings with salt and pepper and fold in the butter to give a nice sauce consistency.

To Serve:
Lightly fry the crab cakes to a golden brown and finish in the oven.

Spoon succotash onto a plate, place the crab cakes around the succotash.

Drizzle the coulis around the crab cakes.

Crab Cake BLT

Memphis Country Club
Memphis, Tennessee

Kenneth Thompson, Executive Chef
Serves 6

Ingredients:

½ cup mayonnaise
1 tsp. Worcestershire sauce
1/8 tsp. Tabasco sauce
½ Tbsp dry mustard
4 Scallions, minced, sautéed
Juice of half a lemon
½ tsp. kosher salt
½ Tbsp. Old Bay seasoning
1 Egg, whole
½ pound jumbo lump crab meat
½ cup bread crumbs
1 qt. Panko bread crumbs, or as needed
½ cup prepared Pesto
½ cup mayonnaise
6 slices of sourdough bread, crust cut off
4 cups baby mixed lettuce
12 slices smoked bacon, cooked
12 slices tomato, sliced ¼" thick

To prepare:

Combine the mayonnaise, Worcestershire, Tabasco, dry mustard, scallions, lemon juice, salt, Old Bay seasoning, and egg in a medium sized bowl. Using a rubber spatula, mix ingredients until fully incorporated.

Add the crabmeat to the mixture and gently fold in. Add the bread crumbs to the mixture and gently fold in.

Place Panko bread crumbs into a shallow pan. Divide the mixture into six portions; form into flat rounds approximately one-half inch thick. Dredge cakes in Panko bread crumbs until evenly coated. Once breaded, place the cakes onto a small sheet pan, cover, and refrigerate until needed.

In a small mixing bowl, combine the mayonnaise and pesto and mix until fully incorporated.

Pre-heat a deep fryer to 325°F. Or put 1/2 inch of oil in heavy saucepan to saute.

Toast each piece of bread until lightly brown.

Place the crab cakes into the pre-heated fryer and cook until golden brown and fully cooked, approximately three minutes.

To serve: start with a piece of the toasted sour dough bread on a plate.

Top with approximately one-half cup of the mixed greens, two slices of the pre-cooked applewood smoked bacon, two slices of tomato, one fried crab cake, and a heaping tablespoon of the pesto mayonnaise.

Serve immediately.

Crab Mac & Cheese

Shula's Hotel & Golf Club
Miami Lakes, Florida

Jamie Fisher, Executive Chef

Serves 4

Ingredients:

3/4 cup Boursin cream

Gemelli pasta, cooked, drained

1 pound jumbo lump crabmeat

1 Tbls Parmesan cheese, grated

1 cup croutons, approx 1/4 inch squares

1 tablespoon green onions, sliced finely

To prepare:

In small sauce pot place boursin cream and bring to a simmer. Add cooked pasta and mix with spoon to combine.

Place in large ramekin, evenly top with crabmeat, then sprinkle with Parmesan cheese, and finally the chopped croutons.

Place in 400° oven on bottom shelf and cook for approximately 7 minutes until top is golden brown and sauce is bubbling.

Garnish with green onions and serve immediately.

Crab Napolean, Avocado and Tomato Salads With Citrus Dressing

Myers Park Country Club Charlotte, North Carolina

Peter Moore, Executive Chef

Serves 4

Ingredients:

For the Avocado Salad:

2 ripe avocados

Juice from one lime

1 tsp chopped cilantro

Salt, pepper and hot
sauce to taste

For the Tomato Salad:

1 lb. ripe seasonal
selection of heirloom
tomatoes

½ small red onion, finely
minced

4 leave fresh basil,
chopped

1 tsp basil oil

Salt and pepper to taste

For the Crab Salad:

4 oz lump crab meat

1 oz mayonnaise

1 Tbls sour cream

Zest and juice from 1 lemon

Chopped parsley

Salt, pepper and Old Bay to taste

To finish the dish:

4 oz jumbo lump crab meat

4 each orange, pink grapefruit Sections
(each piece cut into 3rds)

Dressing of juice from citrus sections with
extra virgin olive oil and chopped chive

Micro green

4 toasted baguette slices

To prepare:

For the Avocado Salad:
Peel and dice 1½ avocados. Mash the remaining
half and lightly fold together. Add the lime juice
and cilantro and season.
Cover with plastic wrap
and refrigerate.

For the Tomato Salad:
Quarter and de-seed the
tomatoes. Cut into ¼ inch dice. Add the remaining ingredients and season to taste.

For the Crab Salad:
Clean the crabmeat and combine with the
mayonnaise and sour cream. Add the remaining items and season to taste.

Final Assembly
Use 3-inch round molds. Place a mold in the
center of a serving dish. Fill one third of the
mold with the avocado mixture and gently
press until flat. (Keep a little avocado mixture
for the final plating). Spoon the tomato salad
on top of the avocado so the two layers fill approximately 2/3rds of the mold.

Complete the tower with the crab salad. Just
prior to service carefully remove the molds
from each tower and present immediately.

73

Crab Cake Tempura
With Mango-Citrus Salad and Ginger Sweet-and-Sour

LaPlaya Beach & Golf Resort
Naples, Florida

Mike Wallace, Executive Chef
Serves 4

Ingredients:

For the crab mix:
1 pound crab meat
2 Tbls sriracha chile sauce*
3 Tbls chives, snipped
2 Tbls mayonnaise
4 Tbls (1/2 stick) butter, melted
2 Tbls ginger, brunoise
1 lime leaf
¼ cup chopped cilantro
1/8 cup chopped mint
Sea salt
Nori sheets
* Available in Asian markets

For the Avocado-Wasabi:
2 avocados, ripe
1 lime, juiced
1 Tbls mayonnaise
1 Tbls wasabi powder
Sea salt to taste

For the Ginger-Lime Gastrique:
2 ounces ginger, finely brunoised
2 cups sugar
1 cup rice wine vinegar
2 limes, juiced

For the Mango Salad:
Mango, julienne
Micro mint or shiso

Wasabi peas
Lime supremes, halved
Orange supremes, cut in thirds

For the Tempura batter:
2 cups flour
2 cups cornstarch
1 Tbls kosher salt
3 Tbls black sesame
1 egg
3 cups soda water

To prepare:

For the crab:
(*Note: the key to this recipe is sourcing the right crab. On the west coast, look for Dungeness; while on the east coast, jumbo lump crab should work. Make sure it is fresh.*)

Pick through the crab and remove any shell fragments. Place crab meat into a clean kitchen towel and aggressively squeeze out any liquid. But do not completely shred the crab or it will ruin the texture.

Melt the butter in a stainless pan over low heat. Add the ginger and the lime leaf and allow to sit for 5 minutes. Remove the lime leaf.

74

Gently fold the remaining ingredients together and season to taste. If necessary, add lime and salt.

Take one sheet of Nori (seaweed wrappers) and place on a clean cutting board with the long side running vertically. Place nine ounces of the crab mix on the bottom part of the nori in a line. When you roll the nori, the two ends should overlap about ¼ inch. If needed, bind with a little water.

Cut the roll into three equal pieces. Don't worry if it gets soggy…the frying will crisp it up again. Repeat until all the crab has been used.

For the Avocado-Wasabi:
Crush ingredients together like making guacamole. Season and add more wasabi as needed.

Sweet Soy:
Boil two cups of soy sauce and 2 cups of brown sugar until large bubbles form and the liquid evenly coats a cold spoon.

For the Ginger-Lime Gastrique:
Cook sugar in a small saucepan until it is evenly caramelized (the color of maple syrup). Add the ginger to the hot caramel. Deglaze with vinegar and lime juice. Cook on low heat until sugar has dissolved and liquid turns a honey-like consistency when put on cold stainless steel.

For the Mango Salad:
Mix all ingredients to order. Mango should be just under-ripe.

For the Tempura batter:

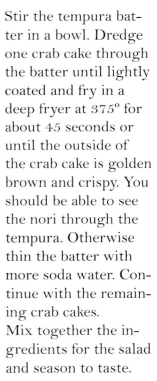

Stir the tempura batter in a bowl. Dredge one crab cake through the batter until lightly coated and fry in a deep fryer at 375° for about 45 seconds or until the outside of the crab cake is golden brown and crispy. You should be able to see the nori through the tempura. Otherwise thin the batter with more soda water. Continue with the remaining crab cakes.
Mix together the ingredients for the salad and season to taste.

To serve:
"Paint" a line of Sweet Soy down the middle of the serving plate on an angle. Trace that line with another of the ginger-lime gastrique so they mingle together.
Arrange the avocado-wasabi on one side of the plate, and the mango salad on the other side in a small pile, topped with a crab cake.

Floribbean Cerviche of Yellowtail Snapper
With Avocado, Palm Hearts and Tomaties

PGA National Resort & Spa
Palm Beach Gardens, Florida
John Sexton, Executive Chef
Serves 8

Ingredients:

For the marinade:

3/4 cup fresh key lime juice
2 Tbls fresh orange juice
1 Tbls olive oil
2 cloves garlic, minced
Freshly chopped chili pepper or jalapeno
1 Tbls freshly chopped cilantro
¼ tsp sea salt
¼ tsp freshly ground black pepper

For the ceviche:

1 pound fresh snapper, ¼ inch dice
1 avocado, cut into ¼ inch dice
1 medium vine ripe tomato, peeled, seeded, and cut into ¼ inch dice
1 heart of palm, sliced into ¼ inch dice
2 Tbls freshly chopped cilantro

Salt and freshly ground pepper to taste
Lime slices for garnish.

To prepare:

Thoroughly mix all the marinade ingredients in a medium bowl.

Fold in the fish, making sure all pieces are coated with marinade. Cover with plastic wrap and marinate in the refrigerator for at least 4-6 hours.

Just before serving, fold in the avocado, tomatoes, hearts of palm and cilantro. Adjust the seasoning, adding more chili peppers if necessary. Serve garnished with lime slices.

76

Florida Lobster Salad
With Asian-Style Noodles
Ginn Hammock Beach Resort
Palm Coast, Florida

Steve Woodard, Executive Chef
Serves 4

Ingredients:

For the Lobster:
4 - 5oz Florida Lobster tails
Butter as needed
Pepper to taste

For the Salad:
½ lb cooked Udon noodles
¼ cup julienne snow peas
¼ cup julienne ginger
¼ cup julienne carrots
¼ cup sliced Shitake mushrooms
¼ cup sliced water chestnuts
1 Tbls toasted black sesame seeds

For the Dressing:
2 Tbls brown sugar
4 Tbls sesame oil
4 Tbls light soy sauce
2 Tbls rice wine vinegar

To prepare:

For the Lobster:
Split lobster tails in half length wise. Discard membrane inside, rinse thoroughly. Top with butter and pepper and roast in a 350° oven until done, about 8-10 minutes. Reserve and cool.

For the Salad:
Combine all ingredients in a bowl, toss with Asian style dressing.

For the Dressing:
Mix all ingredients in a bowl using a wire whisk.

To Plate:
Place noodles in the center of the plate, top with lobster and garnish with scallion sprigs and toasted black sesame seeds

77

Florida-Style Crab Cakes

World Golf Village
St. Augustine, Florida

Scott Zimmerman, Chef
Serves 8

Ingredients:

1 cup yellow onions, diced
1 cup celery, diced
1 cup mixed-color peppers, diced
1 cup green onions
½ cup mayonnaise
¼ cup Dijon mustard
1 tsp Florida Bay seasoning (Old Bay will do)
6 large eggs
1 cup Japanese bread crumbs (Panko)
3 pounds lump crab meat

To prepare:

Sautee yellow onions, celery and peppers until tender and cool. Combine all ingredients, mix well. Refrigerate for 1 hour.

Shape into patties approximately 3 ounces. Sautee over medium heat until golden brown.

Serve hot on bed of greens.

Fried Green Tomatoes
With Tomato Jam and Boursin Cheese
Jasmine Porch at the Kiawah Island Resort
Kiawah Island, South Carolina

Ingredients:

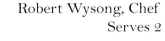

Robert Wysong, Chef
Serves 2

For the tomatoes:
3 slices green tomato, about ¼ " thick
Flour, seasoned with a pinch of salt
Beaten egg
Vegetable oil for frying
3 slices Pancetta, very thinly sliced

Cornmeal breading:
¼ cup yellow cornmeal
¼ cup flour
1 tsp Old Bay
   seasoning

For the tomato jam:
¼ cup sun dried toma-
   toes (rehydrate,
   chop)
2 cups diced roma to
   matoes, fresh
1 Tbls sugar
1 shallot, peeled &
   julienned
1 Tbls cilantro,
   chopped
1 Tbls chili garlic sauce

For the Boursin cheese spread:
2 ounces Boursin cheese
2 Tbls heavy cream
2 Tbls sour cream

To prepare:

For the tomatoes:
Preheat oven to 375°. Place thinly sliced Pancetta on baking sheet lined with parchment paper. Bake until crispy & browned. Cool to room temperature. Dredge sliced tomatoes in seasoned flour, then in beaten egg, then in cornmeal breading. Fry in 4 Tbls hot oil until golden brown on both sides (about 2 minutes).

For the tomato jam:
Combine all ingredients except the cilantro in saucepot and set heat to medium and reduce until it reaches jam consistency. Remove from heat & finish with cilantro; let cool.

For the Boursin cheese spread:
Blend cheese and cream together in mixing bowl until smooth.
To Plate: Place fried green tomatoes on work surface. Top each one with a dollop of tomato jam, a dollop of Boursin cream, then top with a Pancetta crisp.

79

Gateau of Cucumber, Tomato, Spinach and Goat Cheese
With Honey Balsamic Reduction and Dill Sour Cream

Haig Point Club
Daufuskie Island, South Carolina

Bill Bodner, Executive Chef
Serves 4

Ingredients:

For the gateau:
1 cucumber peeled & thinly sliced
12 sliced pole tomatoes
4 ounces spinach (wilted)
4 ounces Goat cheese
Italian Dressing to taste
Mixed greens (as garnish)
Salt & pepper to taste

For the Honey balsamic reduction:
4 ounces Balsamic vinegar
2 ounces honey

For the Dill sour cream:
1 cup sour cream
1 Tbls fresh dill, minced

To prepare:

For the gateau:
Start with one sliced tomato and stack with cucumbers, spinach and goat cheese. Season. Place another tomato slice on top and level off.

Stack and season again, topping gateau with the 3rd slice of tomato.

Repeat for each serving. Keep chilled.

For the balsamic reduction:
Add ingredients to sauce pan and reduce until desired consistency. Remove from heat and let cool.

For the dill sour cream:
Mix ingredients in a stainless bowl. Season with salt and pepper as necessary.

To Plate: On chilled salad plate pool equal portions of the sour cream mixture in the center of the plate. Place the gateau on top. Drizzle with the Italian vinaigrette. Toss the greens in some of the dressing and top the salad. Circle the plate with the balsamic reduction and serve.

80

Grouper Cakes

Atlantic Room at Kiawah Island Resort
St. Augustine, Florida

Randy MacDonald, Executive Chef
Serves 4

Ingredients:

2 lbs fresh cooked grouper
1/2 cup roasted red peppers, small dice
1 avocado, small dice
1/2 cup red onion, small dice
1/4 cup fresh parsley, finely chopped
1 1/2 cups Ritz crackers, crushed
2 tsp white truffle oil
1/2 cup mayonnaise
2 eggs
2 Tbls Cajun seasoning
2 oz Worcestershire sauce
Breadcrumbs for coating the outside

To prepare:

In a mixing bowl, combine all of the ingredients except the breadcrumbs.
Take 3-4 ounces of the mixture and using your hands, form it into the shape of a patty.

Coat the top and bottom with breadcrumbs and sear it on both sides in a sauté pan on medium high until the center is hot.

Hampton Club Shrimp Salad

The Hampton Club
St. Simons Island, Georgia

Allaine Ridenour, Executive Chef

Serves 4

Ingredients:

8 Tiger shrimp, peeled and cooked
1/4 cup red pepper slices
1/4 cup green pepper slices
4 red onion slices
1/4 cup creamy Thousand Island dressing

To prepare:

Mix all ingredients together and serve on a bed of lettuce, Garnish with tomato wedges and garlic crisp pickle.

Lobster Salad Stacker
With Lemon-Dill Dressing
Wilderness Country Club
Naples, Florida

James F. Taylor, Executive Chef
Serves 4

Ingredients:

For the salad:
1 pound fresh Maine lobster meat, diced
½ cup celery, diced
1 tsp fresh dill
¾ cup mayonnaise
Juice of ½ lemon
4 cups mixed greens
1 tomato, diced
1 cucumber, diced
1 yellow tomato, diced

For the dressing:
½ cup sour cream
¼ cup mayonnaise
1 Tbls fresh dill
Juice of 1 lemon

To prepare:

Mix together the lobster meat, celery, dill, mayonnaise and lemon juice and add salt and pepper to taste. Dice the tomatoes and peel and dice the cucumber and wash the mixed greens.

Using a 3-inch stainless steel mold stacker placed in the center of a dinner plate, press in one cup of the greens, followed by ¼ cup of the tomatoes and cucumber. Press ¼ of the lobster salad. Pull the mold up.

Mix the sauce ingredients well together and drizzle on the perimeter of the plate. Garnish with craisens and top with alfalfa sprouts and long chives.

Maine Lobster Club Wrap

Bonita Bay West Club
Bonita Springs, Florida
Xavier Duclos, Executive Chef
Serves 1

Ingredients:

1 tomato tortilla wrap
1 slice of smoked bacon
1/3 tomato, diced
½ cup shredded lettuce
1 lemon
5 ounces lobster salad (see below)

Lobster salad:
Meat from a 1 ¼ Maine lobster
A pinch of chopped tarragon
A pinch of chopped dill
1 tsp capers
1 Tbls sour cream
1 Tbls mayonnaise
1 tsp brandy

To prepare:

Chop lobster meat. Add all the herbs and mayonnaise, sour cream and brandy. Mix all together with pinch of salt and pepper to taste. Stir in capers.

Cook bacon until crispy.

Lay tortilla flat. Add the lobster mix, lettuce, and bacon, and sprinkle tomato on top.

Fold the side of the tortilla and roll tight, cut in half for presentation.

Serve with shoestring potatoes and a wedge of lemon.

Maryland-style Crab Cakes
With Mustard Sauce
Orchid Island Golf & Beach Club
Vero Beach, Florida

Jeff McKinney, F&B Director
Serves 4

Ingredients:

For the crab cakes:
One pound lump crabmeat
1/2 pound jumbo lump crabmeat
2 eggs
1 ½ cups mustard sauce
1 cup panko breadcrumbs
Salt and pepper to taste

For the sauce:
Mix together:
1 cup mayonaise
1 cup Dijon mustard
2 cups sour cream
Juice of 2 lemons
1 Tbls Worchestershire sauce
Salt and white pepper to taste

To prepare:

For the crab cakes:
Mix all ingredients together very gently--do not break up pieces of crabmeat.

Refrigerate for 30 minutes.

Form into 8 4-ounce patties. Pan fry in 4 Tbls canola oil till golden brown.

Serve with side of mustard sauce. At the club we like to serve with sauted fresh spinach and crispy fried onions.

Monica's Chinese Chicken Salad

The Thornblade Club
Greer, South Carolina

Monica Kendrick, Clubhouse Manager
Serves 4

Ingredients:

For the dressing:
¼ cup extra virgin olive oil
7 tbls light sesame oil
2 tbls red wine vinegar
2 tbls sugar
1 seasoning packet from chicken ramen noodles

Mix together in a shaker bottle and set aside

For the salad:
1 large bunch romaine lettuce chopped (or you may use any type of greens you like)
3-4 green onions chopped
1/3 cup roasted slivered almonds
2 Tbls sesame seeds (optional)
3 skinless/boneless cooked chicken breasts chopped
2 pkg uncooked chicken ramen noodles crushed

Mix all ingredients in a large bowl.

Thoroughly shake the dressing and pour over top of salad.

Mix well and enjoy

This salad has been on our menu for at least a year. It is a favorite of men and women alike. It was originally called Chinese Chicken Salad, but when my chef decided to put it on the menu he insisted we call it "Monica's Chinese Chicken Salad" now our club members just say "I'll have a Monica salad"

86

Pecan Chicken Salad
With Spinach and Apple Vinaigrette

Athens Country Club
Athens, Georgia

Christopher McCook, Executive Chef
Serves 6

Ingredients:

6 4–5-ounce chicken breasts, lightly
  pounded and skinned
1 cup bread crumbs, toasted
¼ cup pecans, shelled and roughly chopped
2 whole eggs
¼ cup milk
1 cup seasoned all-purpose flour
2 cups canola oil for frying
Salt and pepper to taste

For the salad:
8 cups spinach, picked and washed
¼ cup tasted pecan pieces
¼ cup chopped cooked bacon
¼ cup mandarin organs
¼ cup crumbled bleu cheese

For the vinaigrette:
2 medium shallots, peeled and minced fine
1 cup olive oil
¼ cup balsamic vinegar
¼ cup apple cider vinegar
¼ cup honey
1 Tbls Dijon mustard
Salt and Pepper to taste

To prepare:

Prepare three bowls, one with the seasoned flour, one with the eggs whisked with the milk and the last with bread crumbs and pecans, seasoned with salt and pepper.

Dip each piece of chicken breast in each of the bowls: flour, egg wash and bread crumbs, then place on a plate and chill. When ready, heat the oil and fry each piece until golden brown. Finish in a 350° oven until the chicken is cooked to an internal temperature of 160°. Keep warm until time to serve.

Toss the salad ingredients together and divide on six plates. Slice the chicken and place on the salad.

Mix vinaigrette ingredients together in a blender. Ladle 2 ounces of dressing atop each salad, reserving some for the side.

Pickled Gulf Shrimp & Bleu Cheese Salad
With local Romaine & Herbed Croutons
Grand Hotel Marriott Resort, Golf Club & Spa
Point Clear, Alabama

Mike Wallace, Executive Chef
Serves 4

Ingredients:

For the Dressing:
2 cups sour cream
½ cup buttermilk
1 Tbls Worcestershire sauce
1 tsp Tabasco sauce
½ lemon, juiced
½ lime, juiced
½ cup caramelized onion
2 cups blue cheese
1 tsp cracked black pepper

For the Salad:
1 head Romaine lettuce
¼ cup shaved red onion
1 cup blue cheese
Kosher salt and cracked black pepper to taste

For the pickled shrimp:
12 U-12 shrimp
2 onions shaved thin
1 tsp celery seed
1 cup olive oil
8 cloves garlic, shaved thin
1 tsp fennel seed

1 tsp mustard seed
1 tsp black pepper
1 tsp coriander

1 Jalapeno pepper (optional)
¼ cup white wine vinegar
½ cup lemon juice

To prepare:

For the pickled shrimp:
Combine all ingredients in a large bowl and toss together.

Cover tightly and let sit for at least six hours to allow the seasonings to set.

Prepare salad and portion on four plates. Add several pickled shrimp and top with dressing.

Savannah Pecan Flounder Salad
With Roasted Red Pepper & Dijon Vinaigrette

**Long Cove Club
Hilton Head, South Carolina**
Leonard Giarratano, Executive Chef
Serves 2

Ingredients:

For the Flounder:
2 flounder filets
2 cups pecans
1 cup Panko bread crumbs
3 Tbls fresh parsley
1 Tbls ground black pepper
Salt to taste
4 eggs, beaten
Flour

For the dressing:
½ pound roasted peppers peeled and
   drained
1 cup cider vinegar
¼ cup whole grain or Creole style mustard
¼ cup Dijon mustard
1 shallot, peeled and chopped
1 Tbls chopped garlic
¾ cup honey
2 tsp kosher salt
1 tsp fine ground black pepper
3 Tbls fresh parsley
1 ½ cups canola oil

For the salad:
1 bag baby spinach
Grape tomato halves
Crumbled goat cheese
Fresh diced golden ripe pineapple
Sliced red onions

To prepare:

For the Flounder:
Grind coarsely together in food processor the pecans, bread crumbs, parsley, salt and pepper. Prepare a small bowl with flour and a separate bowl with 4 beaten eggs. Dip two fillets flounder in flour, then egg, then pecan breading – set aside until ready to cook.
To cook the flounder, pre-heat a small amount of olive oil in a non-stick sauté pan large enough to hold all the flounder laying flat. Brown fish over medium-high heat for 3 minutes per side or until golden brown and crispy. Do not overcook the nut crust.

For the dressing:
In a tall container, combine all dressing ingredients except the oil. Blend with an immersion blender. While continuing to blend, slowly add canola oil until it is fully incorporated.

For the salad:
Arrange spinach on two plates. Garnish decoratively with the tomatoes, pineapples, goat cheese, and onions. Add dressing just before placing the fish on top.

89

Shrimp Caesar Salad

Maggie Valley Club
Maggie Valley, North Carolina

Brian Broderick, Executive Chef

Serves 2

Ingredients:

For the Parmesan Tuile
8 ounces shredded Parmesan cheese

Spread evenly on Teflon coated cookie sheet. Bake in 350° F oven for approximately 3 minutes or until cheese is slightly melted and forms a lattice pattern. Remove from oven. With a 3 inch diameter round cookie cutter, cut cheese into circles. Allow to cool and harden. Set aside.

For the *Croutons:*
2 slices white bread
1 Tbsp melted butter

Take 2 different size round cookie cutters and cut each piece of bread into a donut shape. Center hole of donut shape should be at least 2 inches diameter. Brush melted butter onto top of bread donut. Bake in 350° F oven until golden brown. Set aside.

For the Salad:
1 heart of romaine
6 large cooked shrimp

Caesar salad dressing of your choice
Spring greens for garnish
Tuile
Crouton

Place crouton in center of plate. Holding heart of romaine by the root, dunk completely into the Caesar dressing. Drain excess. Wrap romaine in plastic wrap. Allow to chill in refrigerator for 5 minutes. Remove from refrigerator and cut into 3 inch tall portions. Stand romaine on end and place into center of crouton. Gently remove plastic wrap.

Place parmesan tuile on top. Garnish tuile with spring greens. Top with 3 shrimp. Serve immediately.

Optional: Garnish with Candied Violas

Shrimp Cocktail Salad
With Lemon-Avacado Vinaigrette

Oak Grove Island Golf Club
Brunswick, Georgia

Jackie Grantham, Executive Chef

Serves 4

Ingredients:

For the Shrimp:

8 cups water
2 lemons cut in half
3 bay leaves
2 Tbls whole black peppercorns
1 Tbls Kosher salt
1 tsp Red pepper flakes
1 pound peeled and deveined large shrimp
   with tails intact

For the vinaigrette:

2 lemons
½ cup avocado oil
½ cup canola oil
½ tsp kosher salt
½ tsp Minced fresh garlic
4 turns fresh cracked black pepper

For the Salad:

1 cup micro greens
2 avocadoes
1 cucumber
½ pint Cherry tomatoes

For the croutons:

1 mini French baguette
3 Tbls avocado oil
1 tsp minced garlic
Shaved Parmesan cheese

To prepare:

Shrimp:

Place first 6 ingredients in stockpot. Bring to a boil. Then add shrimp and cover with lid. Turn heat off and let steam for 5 minutes. Drain shrimp in colander and set aside to cool.

Vinaigrette:

In mixing bowl zest 1 lemon. Cut both lemons in half and juice. Add remaining ingredients and whisk all together. Set aside.

Salad:

Place greens in second mixing bowl. Peel and dice avocado to add. Peel cucumber, and then slice in half lengthwise, hull out seeds with measuring spoon and cut into ¼ inch crescent shapes add to greens. Cut cherry tomatoes in half to add. Set aside.

Croutons:

Slice four half-inch wide pieces from baguette. Place oil and garlic in a small mixing bowl. Brush croutons with oil and garlic mixture and toast in heated sauté pan till brown.

To serve: Place 6 cooked shrimp around rim of a martini glass. Toss salad mixture with desired amount of vinaigrette and place in each glass to fill. Top with shaved Parmesan cheese, then top with a toasted crouton slice.

Shrimp, Roasted Onion & Andouille Sausage-Stuffed Tomatoes
With Tomato-Cilantro Puree and Avocado Crema

Emerald Green Private Resort
Tampa, Florida

Kaz Siftar, Executive Chef
Serves 4

Ingredients:

For the stuffing:
1 Tbls olive oil
½ pound shrimp, peeled and deveined
1 onion, julienne
¼ pound Andouille sausage, chopped
¼ cup white wine
2 Tbls Old Bay spice
2 Tbls fresh basil chiffonade
¼ cup Panko bread crumbs

For the tomatoes:
Six tomatoes
2 ounces extra-virgin olive oil
1 pinch ground cumin
Salt and pepper to taste

For the Tomato-Cilantro puree:
1 cup chopped tomatoes
3 scallions, chopped
2 cloves of garlic
Juice of 1 lime
¼ cup cilantro
1 pinch cumin
1 tsp salt and pepper

For the Avocado Crema:
1 avocado, peeled and pitted

1 cup sour cream
2 Tbls lime juice
1 tsp Cayenne pepper
1 tsp cumin
Salt and pepper to taste

To prepare:

For the stuffing:
Heat the olive oil in a sauté pan and add the shrimp, onion, sausage and salt and pepper and cook for approximately 5-6 minutes or until shrimp are browned.
Add the wine, Old Bay sauce, basil and bread crumbs and set aside.

For the tomatoes:
Cut tomatoes in half, scoop out seeds and pulp and lay out on sheet pan. Season each half with olive oil, cumin and salt and pepper. Roast in 400° oven until browned and softened, about 10 minutes. Remove from oven and fill with the shrimp mixture. Serve immediately.

92

SouthWood Grilled Chicken Salad

SouthWood Golf Club
Tallahassee, Florida

Randy McQuaig, Executive Chef
Serves 2

Ingredients:

4 ounces mixed greens
1 ounce dried cranberries
1 ounce chopped walnuts
2 ounces shredded carrots
2 ounces ranch dressing
2 teaspoons horseradish
6 ounces chicken breast, grilled

To prepare:

Toss together first six ingredients. Plate and top with sliced chicken breast. Serve with fresh-baked bread.

Spring Lamb Salad
With Fresh Berries, Gorgonzola Cheese and Citrus Vinaigrette

Haig Point Club
Daufuskie Island, South Carolina
Bill Bodner, Executive Chef
Serves 4

Ingredients:

For the lamb:
2 racks of lamb
1 tsp minced fresh basil
1 tsp minced fresh oregano
1 tsp minced fresh thyme
1 tsp minced fresh rosemary
3 cloves minced garlic
1 Tbls Dijon mustard
3 Tbls salad oil
Salad oil as necessary to sear lamb

For the Citrus Vinaigrette:
1 small shallot minced
1 small garlic clove minced
Juice of 1 orange (seeds removed)
Juice of 2 limes (seeds removed)
Juice of 1 lemon (seeds removed)
3 ounces salad oil
Salt & pepper to taste

For the salad:
12 ounces mixed greens
Fresh raspberries
Fresh blackberries
6 ounces Gorgonzola cheese
Candied Walnuts
For the Candied Walnuts:
1 cup walnuts, halved
2 cups water
1 cup sugar

To prepare:

For the lamb:
Combine all ingredients in a bowl. Set aside. Trim excess fat off the lamb and season with salt and pepper. Coat a skillet lightly with oil and sear the lamb meat side down until golden brown. Remove from pan and coat with the herb mixture. Cook lamb in a 350° oven to desired temperature. Remove from oven and let stand.

For the Citrus Vinaigrette:
Place all ingredients except the salt & pepper into a blender. Blend well and season to taste. Remove from blender and refrigerate until needed.

For the Candied Walnuts: In saucepan add all the ingredients and slowly simmer until sugar mixture is the consistency of thick maple syrup. Strain and deep fry nuts until dark golden brown. Lay flat on parchment paper lined pan and let cool.

To serve: Toss the greens with the dressing and divide equally among 4 chilled plates. Sprinkle with the berries, walnuts and equal portions of the Gorgonzola cheese. Place the warm double cut chops on the salad and serve.

94

Sauces, Dressings & Sides

*O*ur Southern chefs know that a delicious
sauce, dressing or side dish can make a
meal great. Here are a handful of quick and
easy recipes that can dress up a salad or add a
saucy zing to your entree.

95

Carrot and Ginger Dressing

The Golf Club at Briar's Creek
John's Island, South Carolina

David Tolerton, Executive Chef
Makes 1-1.5 quarts

Ingredients:

2 each large peeled chopped carrots
¼-½ cup peeled chopped fresh ginger
1 tsp peeled chopped garlic
2 cups fresh orange juice
1 cup light soy sauce
1 cup rice wine vinegar (white wine, champagne vinegarmay be substituted)
1 large bunch washed cilantro
8 each stalks of chopped green onion
1 tblsp Coleman's dried mustard mixed with 1 tblsp water
½ cup Thai sweet chili sauce
½ cup light brown sugar
1 Tbls Hoi son or oyster sauce
2 Tbls sesame oil
1-2 cups water
Pinch of salt and pepper to taste.

To prepare:

Place ingredients into a blender and blend on high speed until all ingredients are thoroughly combined, season to taste.

Place in air-tight container and refrigerate, will keep for at least two weeks.

This an excellent dressing or dipping sauce for salads, oriental noodles, spring rolls, wontons, steamed chicken or fish and marinated pork tenderloin.

Gorgonzola Salad Dressing

Latitude 31 and Rah Bar
Jekyll Island, Georgia

Dan Dickerson, Chef
Makes about a quart

Ingredients:

1 quart mayonnaise
1 cup sour cream
1 cup onion finely diced
¼ cup garlic, chopped
¾ cup parsley, chopped
1 cup scallions, chopped
2 tablespoons Worcestershire sauce
2 pounds Gorgonzola cheese, crumbled
¼ cup red wine vinegar
1 quart buttermilk

To prepare:

Combine all ingredients in a large mixing bowl and mix thoroughly. Refrigerate immediately.

Peach Pecan Vinaigrette

Pinehurst Resort
Pinehurst, North Carolina

Scott Rowe, Executive Chef
Yield: 1 quart

Ingredients:
1 pound peaches (fresh or frozen)
3 ¼ ounces cider vinegar
1 ¼ ounces Dijon mustard
2 ounces honey
10 ounces corn oil (or oil of choice)
2 ounces chopped pecans

To prepare:
Place all ingredients except oil in food processor and puree.
With processor running, slowly add oil.
Stir in pecans and season with salt and pepper to taste.

Potato Salad Dressing

Wexford Plantation
Hilton Head Island, South Carolina

Frank Copeland, Executive Chef
Yield: About a cup

Ingredients:
1 baked potato
1 tablespoon Dijon mustard
¼ cup red wine, champagne or white wine vinegar
1 clove garlic
3 cups olive oil
Salt and Pepper
Warm water

To prepare:
Place warm baked potato, mustard, vinegar, and garlic into a blender and process until smooth. Slowly add the olive oil.

This dressing will be somewhat thick due to the gluten and starch in the potato. Add some warm water to thin. Season to taste with salt and pepper.

Additional seasoning may be added: fresh chopped chives, roasted garlic or green peppercorns.

Dressing will keep for one week in the refrigerator. Can be served with cooked shrimp, grilled fish or other seafood.

97

Raspberry Vinaigrette

Long Cove Club
Hilton Head Island, South Carolina

Frank Copeland, Executive Chef
Yield: About a quart

Ingredients:
38.5 ounces raspberry dessert sauce
2 cups white vinegar
1 cup red wine vinegar
2 shallots, quartered
1 cup Dijon mustard
1 Tbls Kosher salt
1 cup apple juice
1 ounce fresh mint
6 cups salad oil

To prepare:
Combine all ingredients except the salad oil and blend well with an immersion blender. Continue to blend and slowly add the oil.

Label, date and refrigerate.

Vinaigrette a la Mignonette

The Golf Club at Briar's Creek
John's Island, South Carolina

David Tolerton, Executive Chef
Makes 1-1.5 quarts

Ingredients
1 cup of apple cider vinegar
1 Tbls very finely shallots
1 tsp freshly ground black pepper
Squeeze of fresh lemon
Pinch of sea salt

To prepare:
Combine above ingredients and top freshly shucked oysters.

98

Sauces and Sides
North Carolina
Sweet Potato Hash

The Point Lake and Golf Club
Mooresville, North Carolina

Travis Dale, Executive Chef

Serves 4-6

Ingredients:

1 pound sweet potatoes, peeled, diced & blanched*

1 red onion, peeled, thinly sliced, cooked until golden brown

½ pound applewood smoked, thick cut bacon

1 cup small marshmallows

3 Tbls good maple syrup

2 Tbls toasted pecan pieces

1 Tbls olive oil

1 Tbls unsalted butter

1 Tbls fresh chopped chives

Salt and pepper to taste

To prepare:

Cut bacon into thin strips and render. Cook until semi crisp, drain and discard oil. Place bacon on a paper towel lined plate until service.

In a non-stick skillet heat olive oil to medium-high and add sweet potatoes. Place sweet potatoes in one single layer so that they start to become golden brown (think hash browns). Lightly season with salt and pepper. Be careful not to over season, you will be adding bacon later that will add more salt to your dish.

Add whole unsalted butter once they start to get brown. Toss the potatoes a couple times. Adjust your stove top to a medium heat. Add onion and bacon; continue to cook for a few minutes. Be careful not to burn.

When your hash looks golden brown, add the syrup and chives and cook for a minute. Adjust the seasoning and place in a casserole dish or serving dish. Top with marshmallow and place under broiler until golden.

CHEF'S TIP: Use a propane torch to toast golden brown.

Top with toasted pecans and serve.

*to "blanch"… Peel potatoes and place in cold water so that they do not turn brown. With a sharp knife cut into medium dice (about the size of a marble). Place in a pot of cold water and bring to a boil. They will cook rather quickly. Cook until just soft. Strain off the hot water and run under cold water until cool. Place in the refrigerator, covered until needed. They will keep a couple of days.

Cucumber Jam

The Golf Club at Briar's Creek
John's Island, South Carolina

David Tolerton, Executive Chef
Yield: 1 cup

Ingredients:
1 pound European or hot house cucumbers, peeled seeded and sliced.
2 Tbls salt
2 cups sugar
½ cup dry vermouth
2 Tbls vinegar (malt, cider, champagne, or rice)
1 tsp crushed dried red pepper (optional)

To prepare:
Sprinkle the cucumber slices with a fine layer of salt and let sit for 20 minutes. Place in a colander and rinse under cold running water. Drain on paper towels. Pat dry.

Combine the sugar, vermouth, vinegar and pepper in a small saucepan over medium-low heat. Bring to boil. Add the cucumber slices and return the mixture to a boil. Reduce the heat and simmer for 20-30 minutes, or until mixture reaches the consistency of jam.

Remove from the heat and let cool. Place in air-tight container and refrigerate until ready for use.

This jam pairs well with grilled Fish or a topping on lunch style sandwich (Smoked Salmon or sauté fish)

Green Tomato Jam

The Golf Club at Briar's Creek
John's Island, South Carolina

Ingredients:
2-3 pounds cored and roughly chopped fresh green tomatoes
3-4 cups of granulated sugar
4 cups chardonnay or sweet dessert wine
1 cinnamon stick
Pinch of mustard seeds
1 bay leaf

To prepare:
Place all ingredients into a heavy bottom sauce pot, cook over medium heat stirring occasionally as not to burn. This process may take 45 minutes to 1 hour.

The tomato jam is ready when the liquid has evaporated from the pan and the tomatoes have turned a translucent color.

100

Take of from stove & let cool, store in air-tight containers and refrigerate, this jam will keep for up to 1 month.

Serve the jam with grilled fish, poultry, steaks, pork or during bread service with butter.

Bloody Mary Cocktail Sauce

David Tolerton, Executive Chef
The Golf Club at Briar's Creek
Johns Island, SC

Ingredients:

1 cup ketchup
1 cup chili sauce
¼ cup clam juice
1 cup Zing Zang Bloody Mary mix (or your favorite)
1-2 Shots of Vodka (your preference)
2-3 tblsp prepared horseradish
1 tblsp fresh lemon juice
Couple of dashes of Tabasco
Couple of dashes Worcestershire sauce
Pinch celery salt
Pinch old bay seasoning or K-Paul Blackening spice
Ground black pepper

To Prepare:

Combine all above ingredients in a bowl, adjust seasonings as necessary.
Use with fresh boiled shrimp. Store in airtight container and refrigerate. This will keep for at least one month.

Yields one quart.

Cranberry, Apple & Orange Compote

David Tolerton, Executive Chef
The Golf Club at Briar's Creek
Johns Island, SC

Ingredients:

1 pound fresh cranberries
1-1/2 cups sugar
½ cup fresh orange juice
1 cup sparkling water
2 jars chopped Dutch apples
1 can drained mandarin oranges
1 cinnamon stick
Pinch chopped fresh rosemary-(optional)
One shot Grand Marnier-(optional)

To Prepare:

Place all above ingredients in a heavy duty sauce pot, stir until ingredients are combined. Bring to a boil over medium-high heat, reduce heat to a simmer and stir every 3-4 minutes. Sauce is ready when the cranberries have popped.

Remove from stove, remove cinnamon stick, place in clean container and let cool.
Sauce will thicken as it cools.

Serve with roasted turkey, chicken, pork, game or veal. Store in air-tight container in refrigerator. The sauce will keep for ten days to two weeks.

Yields about 6-8 servings

Summer Mango Relish

Tim Henderson, Executive Chef
The Peninsula Yacht Club
Cornelius, North Carolina

Ingredients:

4 lbs fresh mangoes, diced to ¼ inch
1 oz fresh Jalepeno, diced to 1/8 inch
6 oz red bell pepper, diced to 1/8 inch
¼ cup basil, thin julienne
¼ cup green onion, thin sliced
2 tsp lime zest
2 tsp orange zest
¼ cup lime juice
¼ cup orange juice
1 tbs fish sauce
4 lbs fresh mangoes, diced to ¼ inch

1 oz fresh Jalepeno, diced to 1/8 inch
6 oz red bell pepper, diced to 1/8 inch
¼ cup basil, thin julienne
¼ cup green onion, thin sliced
2 tsp lime zest
2 tsp orange zest
¼ cup lime juice
¼ cup orange juice
1 tbs fish sauce
1 tbs sesame Oil
2 tbs honey
1 tbs canola oil

To Prepare:

Combine all ingredients in large bowl, toss well. Serve over grilled fish with steamed rice.

Tandoori Marinade

David Tolerton, Executive Chef
The Golf Club at Briar's Creek
Johns Island, SC

Ingredients:

3 cups plain low fat yogurt
1 bunch chopped fresh cilantro
1 bunch fresh chopped mint
¼ cup fresh chopped green onions
¼ cup freshly squeezed lemon juice

1 each medium sized green chili pepper, seeded & chopped- pinch cayenne pepper may be substituted. (Wear gloves when working with chili peppers)
½ cup olive oil
1 tbsp fresh chopped ginger
1 tsp ground turmeric,
1 tsp ground cumin
1 tsp curry powder or paste
1 tsp chopped garlic
1 small peeled chopped onion sautéd &

cooled
Salt & ground white pepper to taste

To Prepare:

Place all ingredients into processor and blend on medium/high speed until smooth.
Place marinate in air-tight container and refrigerate. Make a day or two ahead to allow the flavors to infuse.

To marinate poultry, steaks, pork, salmon, shrimp or vegetables, pour over the item, place in an air-tight container and refrigerate overnight. Before baking or grilling a marinated item, wipe off some of the marinade as it can char when cooking.

This sauce will keep for 2 weeks refrigerated. Yields 1-2 quarts.

Traditional Savory Herb Stuffing

David Tolerton, Executive Chef
The Golf Club at Briar's Creek
Johns Island, SC

Ingredients:

1 cup (2 sticks) butter
¼ cup vegetable oil
2 medium Vidalia onions, peeled & finely chopped
¾ lb fresh button mushrooms, chopped
4 stalks celery, chopped
2 cups peeled finely chopped carrot
2 cups cleaned chopped leeks, washed and cleaned
4-6 cloves peeled garlic, chopped finely
1 cup fresh chopped parsley
1 tsp each fresh chopped thyme, rosemary, sage and savory
1 tblsp poultry seasoning
10 cups stale bread, (your choice) broken into ¼" pieces.
5-6 cups low sodium hot chicken broth
2 each beaten eggs
Salt & pepper to taste

To Prepare:

Pre-heat oven to 350 F, butter a casserole dish, a 15"x10" baking dish or a soufflé dish.

Melt butter and oil over medium heat in a large skillet. Add onions, celery, mushrooms, carrots, garlic and leeks. Cook for 3-5 minutes stirring occasionally, add freshly chopped herbs, poultry seasoning and salt and pepper

Place stale bread in large bowl, add vegetable herb mixture. Add the beaten eggs and warm stock a little at a time until the mixture looks moist.

Transfer stuffing mixture into prepared casserole dish, cover with buttered foil and bake in pre-heated oven, for 35-45 minutes until heated throughout.

Soups & Stews

*T*he South is renowned for its wonderful gumbos, stews and soups. We've included several recipes for that Lowcountry delicacy, She-Crab Soup as well as several versions of a filling seafood gumbo.

Asparagus and Brie Soup

The Golf Club at Briar's Creek
John's Island, South Carolina

David Tolerton, Executive Chef
Serves 8-10

Ingredients:

1 large bunch of green asparagus (roughly chopped, green part only no parts of the bottom of the stems)
1 stick butter
¼ cup all purpose flour
6-8 cups chicken or vegetable broth/stock
2 cups heavy cream
1 cup finely chopped white onion
1 cup finely chopped celery
1 cup finely chopped leek
1 tsp chopped garlic
6-8 oz Brie cheese
Salt & Pepper to taste
Dash hot sauce (optional)

To prepare:

Melt butter over medium to low heat in a heavy bottom sauce pot. Add chopped onion, celery, leek, garlic and asparagus. Season with salt and pepper, cook for 5-8 minutes stirring every so often.

Add flour to this vegetable mixture to make a roux which will thicken the soup. Cook the vegetable flour mixture for 2-3 minutes. Add the chicken or vegetable stock, stir consistently till all the stock is added. Bring to a simmer and lower the heat -- be careful not to burn the soup at this stage as the roux can scorch the bottom of the pot.

Add the heavy cream and adjust seasonings with salt and pepper to taste. Simmer for 10-12 minutes, then slowly whisk in the brie a little piece at a time until brie is incorporated into the soup. Blend the soup using a hand stick blender.

Serve in warm soup bowls with crusty bread.

NOTE: For Oyster and Spinach Soup/Bisque, substitute the fresh spinach for the asparagus and add shucked oysters after the soup has been blended.

106

Black Bean & Coconut Milk Soup
With Toasted Coconut and Fresh Lime

Card Sound Country Club
Key Largo, Florida

Kevin Cornaire, Executive Chef
Serves 4-6

Ingredients:

3 16 ounce cans black beans
1 16 ounce can unsweetened coconut milk
1 16 ounce can chicken broth
1 cup chorizo sausage, ground
1 Spanish onion, diced
6 cloves garlic, minced
1 cup coconut, toasted
1 limes, cut into 6 wedges

To prepare:

In a 3 quart sauce pot sauté chorizo until brown, add in onions and garlic and sauté until translucent.

Add 2 cans black beans, coconut milk, and chicken broth. Set heat to medium low and let simmer for ½ hour. Remove soup from heat and puree in small batches in blender.

Do not fill blender more than half way as the heat will cause the liquid to expand.

After all soup is puréed return to pot and add the last can of beans return to a simmer.

Ladle soup into bowls, sprinkle with toasted coconut and lime wedge.

107

Chilled Peach Gazpacho
The Verandah Grill at the Partridge Inn
Augusta, Georgia

Bradley Czajka, Chef
Serves 4

Ingredients:

18 peaches, pitted & chopped
6 ounces honey
8 ounces Peach Schnapps
4 ounces Sherry
1 tsp cinnamon
1 Tbls salt
1 tsp Cayenne
  pepper
2 ounces Lime juice
3 white peaches,
  wedged & grilled
1 tsp garlic,
  minced
1 tsp Jalapeno
  pepper, minced
1 Tbls cilantro,
  chopped
1 tsp mint,
  chopped

To prepare:

Combine the first group of ingredients into a blender and puree until smooth.

Taste for seasoning and adjust as needed. Let sit for at least 3 hours so the flavors meld together.

Grill the white peaches on a hot grill to just mark, let cool.

Finely dice the grilled peaches and combine with the garlic, jalapeno, cilantro, mint and the lime juice. Let the garnish rest for at least an hour for the flavors to come together.

To serve: place 6 ounces of the gazpacho in a martini glass and garnish with the spicy grilled white peach mixture.

108

Crab & Artichoke Bisque

Wexford Plantation
Hilton Head Island, South Carolina

Frank Copeland, Executive Chef
Serves 4-6

Ingredients:

1/4 lb. (1 stick) unsalted butter
1 pound fresh lump crab meat (picked and cleaned of shells)
2 stalks celery, small diced
1 medium onion, peeled and diced
¼ tsp fresh thyme
½ cup flour
6 cups chicken stock or clam juice
2 cups heavy cream
2 small cans of artichokes, chopped
1 bunch green onions, chopped
Salt and pepper to taste

To prepare:

Melt butter in a heavy saucepan over medium heat. Add diced onions, celery, thyme and green onion and cook for 3-4 minutes. Season with salt and pepper.

Add flour, mixing with spoon, and continue to cook for an addition 2-3 minutes. Slowly whisk in the stock, add the chopped artichokes ande cream. Bring the soup to a boil, stirring occasionally. Add the crab meat.
Place the soup in a blender and pulse for a minute or so or use a hand blender. Season to taste.

Serve soup in warm bowls. Fresh corn bread is an excellent accompaniment.

Options: add a cup of fresh or frozen corn kernels; substitute oysters for the crab meat.

PHOTO COURTESY GROG AT WEXFORD PLANTATION

Cream of Three-Onion Soup

Carolina Trace Country Club
Sanford, North Carolina

Martin Shapter, Executive Chef
Serves 6

Ingredients:

4 Tbls extra-virgin olive oil
1 large red onion, julienne
1 large white onion, julienne
1 bunch leeks, julienne
1 tsp thyme
2 Tbls granulated sugar
1 bay leaf
½ tsp coarse sea salt
¼ cup brandy
1 quart chicken stock
1 quart beef stock
1 cup heavy cream
Chopped chives for garnish

To prepare:

Heat the olive oil in a heavy saucepot. Add onions and leeks, sugar and thyme and cook on a low flame until caramelized.

Deglaze with brandy, and add chicken and beef stock. (Canned broth can be substituted if fresh stock is not available.)

Add sea salt and bay leaf and simmer for 30 minutes.

Puree soup in a processor or blender but discard bay leaf first. Add heavy cream and bring back to just a simmer to heat.

Garnish with chopped chives and serve.

PHOTO BY GREG LAMB

Creek Club Clam Chowder

Reynolds Plantation
Lake Oconee, Georgia

Gerald Schmidt, Executive Chef
Serves 8

Ingredients:

24 chowder clams, washed and scrubbed
12 ounces fresh clam liquid (see below)
24 ounces clam juice (canned)
1/8 cup bacon, raw, diced small
¼ cup Vidalia onion, cut fine-dice
¼ cup celery, cut fine dice
3 Tbls all purpose flour
1 cup new potatoes, peeled and cut into
    quarter-inch cubes (place in clean water
    to prevent oxidation)
16 ounces heavy cream
Ground white pepper to taste
Tabasco Sauce to taste
Worcestershire sauce to taste
4 Tbls (½ stick) unsalted butter
Oyster crackers to garnish

To prepare:

With a clam knife, shuck the clams into a stainless steel or glass bowl, retaining meat and juice. Transfer shells into a large sauce pot and add 2 cups of water. Bring to a rapid boil and cover pot with lid. Let stand 15 minutes. Then, slowly pour the liquid through a fine strainer, reserving the cooked stock. (A slightly dampened coffee filter can also be used. Simply dampen with water and place into a strainer and allow the liquid to pass.)

There should be about 12 ounces reserved. Chop the clams to your desired size. I tend to keep them larger than smaller. Separate the meat from the juice and reserve till later.

In a non-aluminum sauce pot over medium heat, render the bacon until it is slightly browned. Cook the onions and celery in the bacon fat for about 5-7 minutes until they appear translucent. Do not caramelize the vegetables, adjusting the heat source if needed.

Add the flour and cook for about 5 minutes, stirring occasionaly to keep from burning. Again, adjust the heat source if needed.

Add the clam juice and clam liquid to the roux mixture. Whisk thoroughly to remove any lumps. Increase the heat and bring to a boil. Continue to stir and prevent any bottom sticking. Reduce to a simmer and cook for approximately 35-40 minutes.

Drain the potatoes, rinse with clean water, and add them to the soup base and continue to simmer until the potatoes are cooked.

Add cream to a separate sauce pan and bring to a quick boil, then immediately remove from heat. Add the cream to the soup and stir. While still simmering, adjust the seasoning with the salt, pepper Worcestershire and Tabasco sauce. Finish with the sweet butter.

To serve: Ladle into warmed soup bowls, garnish with oyster crackers and serve.

111

Daniel Island She-Crab Soup

Daniel Island Club
Charleston, South Carolina

Tyler Dudley, Chef
Serves 4-6

Ingredients:

1/4 pound (1 stick) butter
1 onion, small dice
2 stalks celery, small dice
½ cup all-purpose flour
1 quart lobster or crab stock
1 cup whole milk
½ cup heavy cream
½ cup tomato paste
1/4 cup dry sherry
1 Tbls paprika
2 pounds crab meat
¼ pound crab roe, picked for shells
1 tsp Tabasco sauce

To prepare:

Melt butter over medium heat in stock pan. Add onion and celery and sauté. Add flour to make a roux.

Whisk in hot stock, milk, sherry and cream.

Whisk in paste, paprika and bring to a boil.

Add crab meat and roe, puree and adjust seasoning.

Add Tabasco just before serving.

112

Georgetown Rice Planters She-Crab Soup

Litchfield Country Club
Pawleys Island, South Carolina

Jay Potterfield, Executive Chef

Serves 4-6

Ingredients:

2 quarts clam juice
1 quart heavy cream
2 cups rice
6 cups milk
1 pound back fin crab meat
1 pound claw crab meat
1 yellow onion grated
2 Tbls crab boil/seafood seasoning
1 tsp nutmeg
1 tsp white pepper
Salt to taste
¼ cup sherry
3 hard-boiled egg yolks, diced for garnish

To prepare:

Bring clam juice to a boil. Add yellow onion and all seasonings except salt. Simmer seasoned broth on low.

Bring the rice and 5 cups of the milk to a boil. Reduce to a very low simmer, leave uncovered and stir frequently. When rice is soft and has absorbed most of the liquid remove from heat and allow to cool for 15 minutes. Put cooked rice into food processor or blender with the additional cup of milk and blend until smooth. slowly whisk blended rice into clam broth mixture. Whisk the quart of heavy cream to the mixture and slowly bring the combined ingredients to a boil, while stirring very frequently.

Lower heat to low and allow soup to combine and thicken slightly, about 10 minutes. Add crab meat and sherry. Season lightly with salt to taste. Serve hot and garnish top of each soup with 1 teaspoon of diced hard-boiled egg yolks.

Grilled Chicken and Roasted Red Pepper Soup

Rolling Hills Country Club
Monroe, North Carolina

Larry Henfling, Executive Chef
Serves 4-6

Ingredients:

8 roasted red peppers
1 quart chicken stock
1 stalks of celery, small dice
1 yellow onion, small dice
8 grilled chicken breasts
2 cups heavy cream
2 Tbls garlic, minced
2 Tbls shallots, minced

For the roux:
1/4 pound (1 stick) butter
½ cup all-purpose flour

To prepare:

Make the roux by melting butter in a sauce pan over low heat. Slowly add the flour, stirring continuously until completely incorporated in the butter. Allow to cook for 5 minutes, stirring occasionally. Set aside to cool.

Grill the chicken breasts until cooked and set aside to cool. When cool, dice small and reserve.

Sweat the celery and onions in a little butter until translucent. Add the garlic and shallots and cook for an additional minute. Add the chicken stock and bring to a boil.

Slowly add the roux, stirring constantly, until incorporated. Lower heat to a simmer and cook for 10 minutes. Add the heavy cream and cook for 10 more minutes.

Add chopped roasted red peppers and puree into the soup. Add the diced chicken and season with salt and pepper.

114

Gumbo Ya Ya
With Smoked Chicken and Andouille

Musgrove Country Club
Jasper, Alabama

Phil Schirle, Executive Chef
Serves 6-8

Ingredients:

1 Smoked chicken (2 ½- 3 pounds)
2 ribs celery (rough chop)
1 large onion (rough chop)
1 tablespoon whole black peppercorns
2 bay leaves
 Water
1 cup celery (diced)
2 cups onion (diced)
1 cup green bell pepper (diced)
2 tablespoons garlic (minced)
1 ½ pounds Andouille sausage (thin sliced)
2 ounces Creole seasoning
½ cup dark roux
Blonde roux

To prepare:

Pick the meat off of the smoked chicken.
Discard the skin, save the bones, and dice the
meat and reserve. (You may substitute roasted
whole chickens if you can't get smoked).

Make a stock with the chicken bones, rough
chop celery and onion, the black peppercorns,
bay leaves, and enough water to completely
cover. Simmer, over low flame, for 6 hours,
strain, and reserve the liquid. Discard the
bones.

In a large soup/stock pot, add diced onions,
celery, and bell peppers and sweat ingredients
over medium flame. Cook until vegetables are
wilted. Add garlic and Andouille and cook an

additional 10 minutes over medium heat until
Andouille has started to render.

Add Creole seasoning and toss to coat. Add 3
quarts chicken stock and bring to a boil. Stir
in dark roux, reduce heat to medium, and incorporate until roux is dissolved. Add enough
blonde roux to bring gumbo up to consistency
you wish. Cook until all roux is dissolved into
the gumbo. Stir in reserved diced chicken meat
and simmer an additional 10 minutes.

115

Cajun Kev's Seafood Gumbo

Steelwood Country Club
Loxley, Alabama

Kevin Peters, Executive Chef

Serves 6

Ingredients:

¼ pound all purpose flour
¼ pound (1 stick) unsalted butter
1 qt chicken stock
½ red pepper, chopped
½ yellow pepper, chopped
½ green pepper, chopped
½ medium onion, chopped
4 ribs celery, chopped
1 jalapeno pepper
1 bay leaf
Sprinkle of gumbo file powder
Sprinkle of cayenne pepper
1 Tbls of garlic, minced
1 12 oz can crushed peppers
¼ pound okra
Worcestershire sauce
Basil
Oregano
Tabasco sauce

½ pound andouille sausage, cut into pieces
½ pound 71/90 count shrimp, cleaned
¾ pound crawfish tail meat
¼ pound shucked oysters

To prepare:

Combine butter and flour and cook until smooth and dark brown - almost a foam. Add peppers, onion and celery and cook until soft. Add chicken stock and bring to a boil.

Season with all seasoning except file. Add andouille and seafood and simmer until cooked. Add file and adjust seasoning. Pre-heat skillet and quickly saute sliced okra and add to gumbo.

Serve over cooked white or popcorn rice.

Melon Gazpacho
With Poached Shrimp and Sour Cream
Northwood Country Club
Meridian, Mississippi

Jake Clara, Executive Chef

Serves 4

This recipe is deliciously refreshing and extremely easy because the food processor does 99% of the work for you.

Ingredients:

For the Poached Shrimp:

½ pound peeled and deveined raw shrimp (I use 51-60 count but any size shrimp will work)

1 quart water

½ cup lemon juice

3 tbsp. salt

For the Melon Gazpacho:

2 cups cantaloupe, peeled & seeded, large dice

¼ cup jalapeno peppers, seeded, large dice

½ cup cilantro, chopped

¼ cup shallot, large dice

1 cup white bread, crust removed and large dice

1/3 cup, red wine vinegar

¼ cup extra virgin olive oil

¼ tsp kosher salt

To prepare:

For the Poached Shrimp:

Bring water and lemon juice to a boil in a large saucepan.

Add salt and shrimp. Cook until shrimp are opaque, about 3 minutes.

Drain, let shrimp cool, then dice into bite size pieces.

Bring water and lemon juice to a boil in a large saucepan. Add salt and shrimp. Cook until shrimp are opaque, about 3 minutes. Drain, let shrimp cool, then dice into bite size pieces.

For the Melon Gazpacho:

Place all ingredients into a food processor. (if your processor is not big enough, process in 2 or 3 batches.)

Pulse until all ingredients come together then let the processor run for about 1-2 minutes or until mixture is smooth and combined.

To serve::

Ladle gazpacho into a soup cup or bowl and garnish with a dollop of sour cream and poached shrimp.

117

Midnight Moon Goat Cheese Bisque
With Apple Fennel Relish
Orchid Island Golf & Beach Club
Vero Beach, Florida

Ingredients:

Jeff McKinney, Executive Chef
Serves 4

For the bisque:

1/2 white onion
1 stalk celery
1 peeled carrot
½ bulb fennel
½ turnip peeled
2 tomatoes quartered
½ head of garlic
1 Tbls white peppercorns
4 bay leafs
½ tsp thyme
2 qts cold water
1 tsp salt

For the roux:

¼ pound (1 stick) butter
¼ pound flour

1 quart half and half
1 pound Midnight Moon cheese (or local
   goat cheese)
Salt and white pepper to taste

For the apple fennel relish:

1 Fuji apple
½ bulb fresh fennel
Juice of half lemon
1 tsp olive oil

To prepare:

Place the first ingredients in a stock pot and bring to a boil, then simmer for 30 minutes. Strain and reserve for the vegetable stock.

Thicken the stock with 1/2 pound of blonde roux (quarter pound butter and quarter pound flour cooked until blonde in color)

Bring to boil and add 1 quart of half and half, simmer for 15 minutes.

Add 1 pounds grated goat cheese, stir until smooth and season with salt and white pepper.

For the apple fennel relish:
Fine dice apple and fennel season with lemon, oil. salt and pepper to taste.

To serve: Ladle soup into bowls. Garnish with apple fennel relish.

118

She-Crab Soup

Westin Savannah Harbor Golf Resort & Spa
Savannah, Georgia

Roger Michel, Executive Chef
Makes 2 quarts

Ingredients:
½ fennel head (finely diced)
1 pound onions, diced
1 pound celery, diced
24 ounces pasteurized lump crab meat
Salt & pepper
6 ounces dry sherry
1 quart milk
2 quarts heavy cream

For the Roux
12 ounces (3 sticks) clarified butter
12 ounces (1.5 cups) flour

Saute in milk:
½ ounce fennel seeds

2 bay leaves
¼ ounce black peppercorns
½ ounce parsley stems

To prepare:
Sauté onions, celery and fennel in butter until clear. Add roux. Cook over low heat for approximately 5 minutes.

Add all other ingredients except crab meat. Simmer 20 minutes.

Add crab, adjust seasoning. Serve warm.

119

Shellfish Chowder
TwinEagles Country Club
Naples, Florida

Ingredients:

5 slices finely bacon chopped
1 ½ cups potato, peeled and diced to ¼ inch
½ cup shallot finely chopped
¾ cup clam juice
2 ½ cups whole milk
1/8 tsp cayenne
¼ lb shrimp, shelled, deveined, and cut into ½ inch pieces
½ lb sea scallops, quartered and tough muscle removed
1 tsp salt
½ lb shelled cooked lobster meat, cut into ½ inch pieces
½ lb lump crab meat
2 Tbls chopped fresh cilantro
2 Tbls chopped fresh chives

To prepare:

Cook bacon in a 5-quart heavy pot over moderate heat, stirring occasionally, until crisp, approximately 5 minutes.

Remove ½ the bacon and place on paper towel.

Pour off all but 1 tablespoon fat from pot and add potatoes, shallots, and clam juice.

Simmer covered until potatoes are tender and most of the clam juice is evaporated, approximately 8 minutes.

Add milk and cayenne and return to a simmer.

Add shrimp, scallops, and salt and return to a simmer stirring occasionally until shellfish is cooked through, approximately 3-5 minutes.

Add lobster and half of the herbs and simmer 1 minute.

Serve chowder topped with remaining bacon and herbs.

Spicy Blue Crab Bisque

Steelwood Country Club
Loxley, Alabama

Kevin Peters, Executive Chef
Yield: 1 gallon

Ingredients:

5 pounds Gumbo crabs
2 pounds Mirepoix (chopped onions, celery and carrots)
1 can tomato paste
Bay leaves
Thyme
Brandy
Lemongrass
Red Thai curry

To prepare:

Make a crab stock by roasting the gumbo crabs with mirepoix and tomato paste. When the crabs turn bright red, remove from the oven and flame with brandy.

Place in stock pot and add water, thyme, bay leaves and lemongrass. Simmer the stock for 2-3 hours.

Strain stock into a 10-gallon pot and bring to boil. Add curry and thicken with beurre manger.

Finish with cream and adjust seasoning. Strain again through a chinoise before serving.

121

Sweet Potato Bisque

The Pinehurst Resort
Pinehurst, North Carolina

Scott Rowe, Executive Chef
Serves 4

Ingredients:

3 sweet potatoes (peeled and rough cut)
1 yellow onion (rough-cut)
1 leeks (cleaned & rough cut)
3 ¼ cups chicken stock
¾ cup heavy cream
¾ cup sweet potatoes (medium diced & blanched)
Salt & pepper to taste
1 tsp butter

To prepare:

In 3-gallon soup pot, sweat onions and leeks in butter until translucent.

Add rough-cut potatoes and chicken stock and simmer for 1 hour.

Puree in blender, and return to soup pot.

Add cream, diced potatoes and season.

Tomato Bisque

The Naples Beach Hotel & Golf Club
Naples, Florida

Marwan Kassem, Executive Chef

Serves 4

Ingredients:

6 medium tomatoes, cut in wedges
¼ cup chopped onions
1 zucchini, cut in pieces
1 yellow squash, cut in pieces
½ green pepper, cut in pieces
1 cup canned diced tomatoes
1 stalk of celery, cut in pieces
3 cloves garlic
¼ cup extra virgin olive oil
½ quart heavy whipping cream
1 tsp Tabasco sauce
3 cups water
Salt and pepper to taste
1 bunch chopped basil

To prepare:

Preheat the oven to 375°.

Combine all the vegetables in a roasting pan and drizzle with the olive oil. Roast for 20-30 minutes.

Place the roasted vegetable into a large saucepan, add water and boil for 12-15 minutes. Add the whipping cream and Tabasco sauce and cook for 30 minutes more on medium to low heat. Puree the mixture in a blender approximately 2-4 cups at a time or with a handheld blender.
Pour the pureed soup back into the sauce pan and heat to desire temperature.

To serve: Place in a soup bowl and garnish with diced tomatoes, croutons and chopped basil.

© The Naples Beach Hotel & Golf Club

Entrees

*F*rom delicious crab cakes to yellow tail snapper, the chefs at the fine golf resorts and clubs in the Southeast have outdone themselves in delicious creativity. Any one of these delectable dinners will make a golfer smile, whether he just shot 69 or 110!

Meat Dishes

Beef Braciole

Arnold Palmer's Bay Hill Club & Lodge
Orlando, Florida

Robert Lee, Executive Chef

Serves 4

Ingredients:

2 Tbls chopped parsley
1 pound beef round, thinly sliced
8 slices prosciutto
1 Tbls pine nuts
2 Tbls grated Parmesan cheese
2 chopped garlic cloves
½ cup diced onions
½ cup diced carrots
1 cup red wine
2-28 oz. cans diced tomatoes
¼ cup tomato paste

1 Tbls chopped basil
Salt and pepper to taste

To prepare:

Mix together the pine nuts, cheese and parsley. Spread this mix evenly over a piece of prosciutto placed on a piece of the sliced beef. Roll each individually and secure with toothpicks.

Brown over medium heat in a skillet and remove. Add garlic, onions and carrots to the pan and cook for 5 minutes.

Add wine, the remaining ingredients and the pieces of browned beef and simmer until tender, approximately 1 ½ hours. Serve with your favorite pasta.

Beef Tangine
With Prunes and Sesame Seeds
Club Med Sandpiper
Port St. Lucie, Florida
Erik Peters, Executive Chef
Serves 5

Ingredients:

2 pounds beef, cut into 2" cubes
1/2 whole carrot, minced
1/2 stalk celery, minced
1/4 whole onion, minced
2 Tbls tomato. paste
2 cups beef stock
1 cup water
1 tsp ginger
1 Tbls paprika
1 Tbls cumin
1/2 tsp curry powder
1 tsp coriander
½ tsp cinnamon
4 sprigs fresh cilantro. chopped
½ pound prunes
1 Tbls sesame seeds
2 Tbls olive oil
Salt and pepper to taste

To prepare:

In a medium stock pot, over medium-high heat, add the olive oil and let it get very hot.

Rinse the meat in cold water and pat dry. Once the oil is hot, add the meat, vegetables, 1 tsp of salt, and all the spices except for the cinnamon.

Cook until all the meat is seared, this will take approximately 6-8 minutes. Once the meat is seared, add the stock, water, and tomato paste.

Bring to a boil, reduce to a simmer and cook for approximately 90 minutes, stirring occasionally. The meat should be tender and break apart easily. The liquid should be reduced to form a sauce on its own. After 80 minutes of cooking, add the prunes and cinnamon.

The prunes should cook for no longer than 10 minutes. Remove from heat, sprinkle the sesame seeds and cilantro on top and serve immediately.

Serving Ideas: Serve with couscous.

NOTE: This dish is made with prunes which are one of the classic garnishes for beef in the Moroccan style of making beef stew. There are also hundreds of other garnishes that can be used instead of the prunes. The prunes can be replaced with any other dried Mediterranean fruits such as figs or dates. Another classic garnish would be with artichoke hearts and peas.

Beer Braised Beef Brisket

Croasdaile Country Club
Durham, North Carolina

Tim Gauldin, Executive Chef

Serves 6-8

Ingredients:

One 6 to 7 lb. beef brisket, trimmed
1 cup black pepper, course ground
Salt to taste
4 Tbls olive oil, more if necessary
2 large onions, quartered
4 large carrots, rough chopped
4 celery ribs, chopped
5 whole cloves of garlic, peeled
2 cups or 2 bottles of beer, Pale ales,
    Porters and Stouts preferred
4 cups of a quality beef stock
1 cup of demi-glace
Flour for making gravy

To prepare:

Preheat oven to 325°

Clean the excess fat from the brisket and liberally coat each side with the cracked black pepper. Add desired amount of salt to each side of the brisket.

Heat oil over moderate heat and add the vegetables, minus the garlic. Cook the vegetables for 5 to 7 minutes. Once the vegetables have started to release their aroma push to the sides of the skillet and sear the brisket on each side. The meat should resemble a nice caramel color with no visible red remaining. Place the brisket and vegetables in a roasting pan then pour the beer over the meat. Add the stock and the garlic cloves.

Cover the roasting pan with foil and place in the oven. Bake for approximately 3 hours. Remove from oven and place brisket aside to rest. Meanwhile strain out the liquid (reserve vegetables for garnish) and return the liquid to a skillet. Bring to a boil and slowly add flour then whisk to make gravy.

To serve slice the brisket and top with gravy. Serve with your favorite mashed potatoes and a seasonal vegetable.

Braised Lamb Shanks

Rosen Shingle Creek Resort
Orlando, Florida
James Slattery, Executive Chef
Serves 6

Ingredients:

6 lamb shanks, patted dry
2 cups vegetable oil
1 orange
1 lemon
2 cups all-purpose flour
2 Tbls salt
2 Tbls pepper
5 cloves garlic, crushed
1 cup onion, medium diced
½ cup celery, medium diced
½ cup carrot, medium diced
½ cup tomato paste
1 quart dry red wine
1 quart beef broth
1 bay leaf
2 Tbls chopped parsley

To prepare:

Preheat over to 325°.

Zest the orange and lemon with small channel knife or vegetable peeler, being careful not to use any of the bitter white pith. Set aside.

Place roasting pan on the stove top over medium heat, add the vegetable oil. Season lamb shanks with salt and pepper and dredge lightly with flour on all sides. Brown shanks in the hot oil until browned on all sides. Remove from pan, set aside and add crushed garlic to the pan and lightly brown. Immediately add the onion, celery and carrot. Carmelize until brown, approximately 7 minutes. Add tomato paste and deglaze for approximately 5 minutes.

Add citrus zest, red wine, beef broth, bay leaf and browned lamb shanks to the roasting pan. Cover with aluminum foil and braise in the oven until tender, approximately 2 hours. Gently rotate lamb every 45 minutes to ensure even cooking. Shanks should be tender but not falling apart.

Remove the lamb to a serving plate and discard the bay leaf. Carefully pour sauce into a food processor or blender and puree. The sauce should be thick enough to coat the back of a spoon.

Pour the sauce over the lamb shanks and garnish with parsley. Serve with sweet potato mashed and roasted root vegetables.

Carolina Stuffed Pork Loin

Pine Lake Country Club
Charlotte, North Carolina
Ken Snyder, Executive Chef
Serves 4-6

Ingredients:

Whole fresh pork loin
1 medium onion, sliced thin
1 bunch fresh leaf spinach
12 ounces ground sausage
1 cup plain bread crumbs
1/4 pound (1 stick) butter, softened
1/3 cup dry vermouth
1/3 pound thin sliced honey smoked ham
2 eggs

To prepare:

For the carmelized onions and spinach:
In saute pan melt half a stick of butter on medium-high heat. Add onions and cook till browning occurs, approximately 20 minutes. Add spinach and vermouth, and cook 3 to 4 minutes.

For the sausage:
Brown sausage in a medium sauce pan. Drain grease.

For the pork loin:
Rinse pork in cold water and split ¾ lengthwise and again on the heavy side. Flatten out with meat mallet with fat side down.

To assemble:
In large mixing bowl, combine onions, spinach, sausage, bread crumbs, and softened butter and mix well. Add salt and pepper to taste.

Add eggs and mix again.

Lay out pork fat side down. Season with salt and pepper. Spread the onion and spinach mixture over half the pork loin, leaving 1 inch on both sides with no spread. Add a thin layer of ham on top of the spread.

Slowly roll the pork up, pushing in on the sides. Tie with twine or roll up in heavy-duty foil (If using foil, spray first with nonstick cooking spray so it won't stick to pork).

Place on broiler pan with drip pan, cover and roast at 325° for 90 minutes. If roasting uncovered, add water to drip pan often.

Finish at 150°. Let rest 10-15 minutes before serving.

Cuban Grilled Pork Chops
With Mango, Papaya and Rum Glaze and Mango-Watercress Salsa

Broken Sound Club
Boca Raton, Florida
Joe Longo, Executive Chef
Serves 6

Ingredients:

6 ~ 10 oz center-cut pork chops.

For the Glaze:
3 Tbls olive oil
4 Tbls shallots, minced
2 Tbls garlic, minced
1 tsp ground cumin
1 tsp freshly ground black pepper
2 tsp curry powder
1 cup fresh mango juice
½ cup papaya puree
½ cup dark rum
2 cups chicken stock
3 Tbls molasses

For the Mango-Watercress Salsa:
2 Tbls canola oil
2 medium onions, thinly sliced
½ cup chopped scallions
2 mangoes, peeled and sliced
½ cup fresh lime juice
1 bunch watercress, trimmed
½ cup chopped cilantro
Salt and pepper to taste

To prepare:

For the Glaze:
Heat oil in a saucepan over medium heat; add shallots and garlic; sauté until golden. Add spices; sauté for 3 minutes.

Remove from direct heat and carefully stir in mango juice, papaya puree and rum.

Return to heat; add stock and bring to a simmer. Stir in molasses; reduce to a glaze (about 30 mins), remove from heat and let cool.

Brush pork chops with glaze and refrigerate for at least two hours

Remove chops from refrigerator and grill on both sides until done (about 10 mins on each side), brush with glaze as they cook, transfer to plate.

For the Mango-Watercress Salsa:
Combine oil, onions, mangoes, watercress, cilantro, scallions and lime juice and season.

To servee: arrange a chop in the center of each plate; garnish with warm salsa.

130

Gristmill Surf 'n' Turf
With Hollandaise
Circlestone Country Club
Adel, Georgia

Oscar Orsini, Executive Chef
Serves 4-6

Ingredients:

8 oz. Filet Mignon, per serving
4 ~ 16/20 shrimp
2 slices of bread
1 pound (4 sticks) of clarified melted
   butter
½ tsp minced garlic
8 egg yolks
1 Tbls white wine
1 tsp lemon juice
4 drops Tabasco
   sauce
Salt and pepper to
taste

grilling your filet, sautee shrimp with garlic and 1 tbsp. butter for 3 minutes.

Toast points:
Toast the bread slices and cut into triangles, then place on a plate overlapping each other.

Place filet on plate atop the toast points, then place the shrimp on top of the filet.

Finish off the dish with the hollandaise sauce poured on top.

To prepare:

To make hollandaise sauce:

In a bowl combine egg yolks, lemon juice, white wine, pinch of salt and pepper, Tabasco sauce and melted butter.

Place bowl over pot of boiling water and whisk vigorously until thickened. Set aside until steak and shrimp are done.

Steak and Shrimp:
Rub filet with oil and salt and pepper. Char grill filet to your desired temperature. While

WINE RECOMMENDATION: A nice fruity Cabernet.

131

Hoisin Glazed Pork Ribs
With Mango-Wasabi Slaw
Atlantic Room at Kiawah Island Resort
Kiawah Island, South Carolina

Randy MacDonald, Executive Chef

Serves 4-6

Ingredients:

For the ribs:

2 whole racks St Louis-style pork ribs
(spare ribs minus the brisket bone)

For the rub:

¼ cup 5 spice powder
2 Tbls paprika
1 Tbls hot smoked parika
Pinch red pepper flakes
½ cup brown sugar
¼ cup kosher salt
1 tsp fresh ground szechuan pepper (may
substitute black pepper)

For the sauce:

1 Tbls minced garlic
1 tsp minced ginger
1 tsp sesame oil
1 cup chicken stock (or low sodium canned
chicken broth)
1/3 cup hoisin sauce
1 Tbls soy sauce
2 tsp Chinese fermented black beans (found
in Asian markets,omit if unavailable)
1 Tbls honey
2 tsp miso (found in Asian markets,omit if
unavailable)
1 Tbls chili-garlic paste (found in Asian
markets, omit if unavailable)
¼ bunch cilantro-leaves washed and
chopped(about 2 Tbls minced)
¼ cup ketchup

For the slaw:

½ head Napa cabbage sliced fine (use
electric slicer if possible)
¼ head red cabbage sliced fine
1 red onion sliced fine julienne
1 red pepper-sliced fine julienne
2 vine-ripened tomatoes skin
julienned (core and quarter
tomatoes, run knife just under skin leav
ing ¼-inch of outer flesh)
1 cucumber peeled and julienned fine and
patted dry-flesh only, no seeds
½ jicama-peeled and julienned fine
1 bunch cilantro-leaves only-washed and
julienned fine
approx 3- 4 cup slaw dressing (see below)
1 Tbls sriracha chili paste (found in Asian
markets, omit if unavailable)
2 Tbls honey
2 semi firm mangoes-peeled, pitted and
julienned

For the slaw dressing:

1 English cucumber
2 Tbls rice wine vinegar
1 Tbls fresh lemon juice
1 shallot-minced
1 Tbls honey
¼ cup wasbabi powder
3 cups mayonnaise
Salt and pepper to taste

To prepare:

For the rub:
Combine all ingredients and thoroughly rub down ribs (reserve any excess) and allow to sit at room temp at least 1 hour.

For the sauce:
Saute garlic and ginger in sesame oil. Add everything but cilantro and simmer 30 minutes. Add cilantro and puree.

For the ribs:
Place ribs on grill for a few minutes to give grill marks, then wrap in foil.

Place ribs in deep pan large enough to accommodate them (cut in half if necessary), elevating ribs from bottom of pan with pie racks or improvise by fashioning "rods" of aluminum foil placed in bottom.

Mix 1 quart water with ¼ cup soy sauce and add to pan.

Cover pan with foil and bring to boil on stovetop. When liquid boils, place pan in low oven at 200° for approx 6 hrs or until tender. Brush with sauce, broil briefly, cool and then cut into 2 rib portions.

For the slaw:
Combine all ingredients and adjust seasoning to taste.

For the slaw dressing:
Peel cucumber and reserve skin.

Dice cucumber skin fine, split cucumber lengthwise and scrape and discard seeds from center.

Puree cucumber flesh with vinegar, lemon juice, honey and wasabi powder. Fold in mayo, diced skin and shallots. Season to taste.

To finish:
Brush ribs with additional sauce and broil briefly to reheat.

Drizzle additional sauce on one side of plate and stack or criss-cross 3 ribs on top.

Place small pile of slaw on other side of plate.

Garnish with sesame seeds and minced scallions if desired.

Forsyth Rib Eye
Applewood Bacon-Crusted with Crispy Onion Rings
Forsyth Country Club
Winston-Salem, North Carolina

Michael Mort, Executive Chef
Serves 4

Ingredients:

For the "crust"

4 ounces applewood-smoked bacon, uncooked and small diced
1 clove garlic, finely minced
1 ounce bacon drippings
1 tsp thyme, finely chopped
1 tsp parsley, chopped
2 ounces virgin olive oil
1 cup Panko bread crumbs
½ tsp hot sauce (Texas Pete or Tabasco)
½ tsp ground black pepper

For the onion rings:

1 large yellow onion, peeled and sliced into very thin rings
1 cup buttermilk
Canola oil for deep frying
1 cup all-purpose flour

4 ~10-ounce center-cut rib eye steaks
Kosher salt and pepper to taste
1 shallot, peeled and finely minced
4 ounces hot demi-glace
2 ounces Cabernet wine
1 tsp Dijon mustard
2 ounces Canola oil

To prepare:

Saute the diced bacon in a heavy sauté pan over medium heat until brown and crisp. Drain well and reserve the drippings.

In a food processor, pulse the bacon, garlic, olive oil and 1 ounce of reserved bacon drippings until smooth. Transfer to a stainless steel mixing bowl and combine with thyme, parsley, bread crumbs, hot sauce and pepper. Reserve.

Combine the onion rings and buttermilk in a stainless steel bowl. Drain the onions.

Heat oil in a deep fryer or heavy sauce pan to 365°. Lightly coat the onion rings in flour and fry until golden brown. Remove and drain on paper towels. Keep warm until needed.

Preheat oven to 425°.

Heat oil in heavy sauté pan until hot. Sear steaks for 2 minutes on each side for medium rare. Remove steaks from pan and place in an oven-proof baking dish.

Drain off cooking oil and return pan to medium heat.

134

Add shallots and sauté for about 1 minute—do not allow to brown. Add the Cabernet and reduce by ½ until syrupy.

Add the demi-glace and bring to a simmer, lightly stirring and blending the particles from the bottom of the pan.

Remove from heat, strain and blend in the mustard and adjust seasoning. Keep warm. (Sauce should be thick. Add some hot beef stock if necessary.)

Top each steak with the bacon crust and press firmly.

Place in preheated oven for approximately 5 minutes until crust is light brown. Place on four warmed plates and serve with the reserved sauce and top with onion rings.

Guava BBQ Pork Tenderloin
With Vanilla Guanaban Sweet Potato Mash

Card Sound Country Club
Key Largo, Florida

Kevin Cornaire, Executive Chef
Serves 4-6

Ingredients:

2-3 pounds pork tenderloin
16 ounces guava juice
1 cup mustard base gold barbecue sauce
6 vanilla beans
24 ounces guanabana juice (can be found in Hispanic section of grocery store)
3 pounds sweet potatoes
½ cup dark brown sugar
¼ pound (1 stick) unsalted butter (softened)
Salt and pepper to taste

To prepare:

For the barbecue sauce:
Reduce Guava juice over medium heat until about 4 ounces remains. Add gold barbecue sauce and mix together.

For the sweet potatoes:
Roast sweet potatoes in 350° oven for about 35-45 minutes or until fork tender. Let cool just long enough till they can be handled to peel.

While potatoes are cooling split vanilla beans and scrape the seeds from within. Steep the seeds in the guanabana juice over medium heat until about six ounces remain.

Remove from heat and fold in butter and brown sugar. Cut ends off the sweet potatoes and squeeze potatoes from the skin into a large mixing bowl. Whip vanilla mixture into the potatoes and season to taste with salt and pepper.

For the Pork:
Season pork tenderloin with salt and pepper and grill over a medium hot fire for about 15 minutes (rotating often to insure proper cooking). Brush with barbecue sauce and cook an additional 5 minutes or until an internal temperature of 145° is reached.

Slice and serve with the sweet potato mash.

136

Lobster Stuffed Beef Tenderloin

Enterprise Country Club
Enterprise, Alabama

Clayton B. Rushdon, Executive Chef

Serves 4

Ingredients:

4 ~ 8 ounce filets of prime beef tenderloin

For the Stuffing:
1 Maine lobster tail, steamed (can use canned meat)
¼ pound (1 stick) drawn butter
2 cloves of fresh garlic, finely chopped
2 Tbls chopped chives
1 Tbls fresh dill

½ cup bread crumbs
2 large eggs
Salt and pepper to taste

To prepare:

Finely chop the steamed lobster tail meat. Add remaining stuffing ingredients and blend well (set aside a small amount of dill weed and chives for later).

Butterfly the beef filets and season lightly with salt and pepper.

Preheat oven to 350°.

Place 2 heaping Tbls of stuffing mixture on one side of each filet and fold remaining side over to cover the stuffing. Brush broiler pan with extra virgin olive oil.

Place stuffed filets on oiled broiler pan and brush the tops of each filet lightly with extra virgin olive oil, sprinkling remaining dill weed and chives on top.

Place in oven and bake for 35-40 minutes. Remove from oven and let rest for 5 minutes.

This dish is best complimented with a lemon and dill rice pilaf, and steamed early pea pods.

Medallions of Veal with Oysters

Musgrove Country Club
Jasper, Alabama

Phil Schirle, Executive Chef
Yield: 1 serving

Ingredients:

2 2-ounce medallions of veal
6 oysters
1 shallot, minced
1 cup mushrooms (your favorite)
Brandy, splash
1 ounce red wine
¼ cup demi-glace
2 Tbls butter
Flour
Salt and pepper to taste.

To prepare:

Season the veal medallions with salt and pepper and dust with flour. Saute in butter until brown, then remove and reserve.

Add the shallots and mushrooms to the pan and deglaze with the brandy. Add the red wine and reduce by 90 percent. Add the demi-glace. Add the oysters to the pan and poach until lips just begin to curl, then remove and reserve.

Continue cooking the sauce until it thickens. Add the butter and whisk into the sauce.

To plate: Place veal medallions in center of plate. Cover with sauce and place oysters around the edge.

Mustard-Crusted Lamb Chops
With Cranberry Chutney and Rosemary Lamb Glace
Athens Country Club
Athens, Georgia

Christopher McCook, Executive Chef
Serves 4

Ingredients:

4 Colorado lamb chops, rinsed and dried
2 ounces olive oil
2 garlic cloves, crushed
¼ tsp rosemary, slightly chopped and crushed
1 Tbls wholegrain mustard
1 anchovy fillet, chopped

For the crust:
2 ounces Dijon mustard
3 ounces Panko bread crumbs
1 Tbls wholegrain mustard
1 ounce olive oil
1 Tbls chopped parsley

For the chutney:
2 ounces cranberries
3 ounces sugar
1 orange, juiced
1 Tbls chopped chives

For the glace:
1 quart lamb stock
1 ounce shallots, chopped
2 garlic cloves, crushed
3 stems thyme with leaves
1 ounce port wine
2 Tbls butter

To prepare:

Mix together the olive oil, garlic, rosemary, mustard and anchovy and marinate the lamb chops for one hour.

In a hot pan, slowly brown the lamb chops to desired temperature. Rub the presentation side with Dijon mustard and top with the bread-crumb-mixture.

For the chutney:
Cook the cranberries, sugar and orange juice for 15 minutes. Add orange zest, cool and add chives.

For the glace:
Reduce all ingredients except the wine and and butter to sauce consistency. Add the wine and bring to a high simmer, then add the butter. Strain and serve.

To serve: Broil the crusted lamb chops briefly until golden brown. Drizzle with the glace and add the chutney on the side. Serve with garlic mashed potatoes.

139

Northern Italian Pot Roast
With Grilled Eggplant & Ricotta Fritters

Orchid Island Golf & Beach Club
Vero Beach, Florida
Jeff McKinney, Executive Chef

Serves 6

Ingredients:

3 lb. beef chuck roast
1 can whole tomatoes, crushed
1 onion diced
3 cloves garlic peeled and sliced
1 bay leaf
1 Tbls fresh thyme
1 stalk celery diced
1 carrot diced
2 Tbls tomato paste
1 cup beef broth
1 cup veal glace
1 cup red wine
¼ cup olive oil for cooking

1 pint ricotta impastata (drained or dry
   ricotta cheese)
1 egg yolk
1 egg
1 cup panko breadcrumbs
1 cup a.p. flour
2 Tbls parmesan cheese
Canola oil for frying

1 eggplant peeled and sliced ¼ inch thick

To prepare:

Using butchers twine truss the beef roast,
season with salt and fresh cracked pepper and
sear in olive oil in a dutch oven or large roasting pot until well browned. Add the celery,
onion, carrot, garlic and the bay leaf. Season
and sauté for 3-4 minutes. Add the red wine
and the tomatoes and simmer for 5 minutes.
Add the paste, beef stock, veal glace and
thyme and return the roast back to the pot.
Cover and cook for approximately 3 ½-4 hours
at
250°, or until fork tender.

In a bowl combine the egg yolk, parmesan
cheese, salt and fresh pepper to the ricotta
cheese and mix well. Whisk the whole egg in
a small bowl. Add the flour to a small bowl
and season with salt and pepper. Add the
breadcrumbs to a small bowl and season with
salt and pepper. With a 2 oz. ice cream scoop
or a spoon, scoop small round balls of the
ricotta mixture. Dredge the balls in the flour
dip into the egg wash, and finally coat with
breadcrumbs. Fry in 350° oil for three minutes
or until golden brown.

Season the eggplant slices with olive oil, salt
and fresh cracked pepper. Grill two or three
minutes on each side until tender.

Serve the pot roast with lots of the braising
juices, the eggplant and garnish with the fried
ricotta fritters.

Osso Bucco

Delray Dunes Golf & Country Club
Boynton Beach, Florida

Mark LaFrance, Executive Chef
Serves 6

Ingredients:

6 veal shanks (1 ½" thick)
1 cup onion,fine dice
1 cup celery,fine dice
1 cup carrots,fine dice
2 cloves chopped garlic
1 Tbls rosemary (fresh or dry)
1 Tbls thyme (fresh or dry)
6 cups chicken or beef broth
1 can chopped tomatoes
2 Tbls tomato paste
4 bay leaves
Salt & pepper to taste
Flour
Oil

To prepare:

Preheat the oven to 350°.

Dredge veal shanks in seasoned flour. Sear in hot skillet in oil for 2 minutes each side. Place shanks in baking dish.

Cover with diced carrots, onions, celery, tomatoes, all spices and cover all with the stock. Cover with foil and cook for 2 hours. Remove shanks & bay leaves. Thicken and season the sauce if needed. Pour sauce over shanks in serving dish.

Reheats well.

Roast Pork Tenderloin
With Dried Fruit and Blackberry Demi-Glace

Athens Country Club
Athens, Georgia

Christopher McCook, Executive Chef
Serves 4

Ingredients:

½ pound pork tenderloin, trimmed, split
  open and lightly pounded out
1 cup dried fruit—apricots, cranberries,
  raisins, etc.
3 ounces port wine
¼ cup shallots, minced
½ tsp cinnamon
¼ tsp fresh ginger, grated
1 Tbls butter
2 whole eggs, beaten
1 cup cubed bread—
  baguette, boule, etc.
Salt and black pepper
  to taste

For the blackberry demi-glace
1 cup sugar
2 cups frozen or fresh
  blackberries
1 cup orange zest
¼ cup fresh orange
  juice
1 cup chicken stock

onto the center of the pork, leaving about two inches around the edge. Roll and tie the roast. Sear in a hot pan and all sides, place on a roasting rack and roast at 325° for about 20 minutes, or until internal temperature reaches 160°. Remove from oven and allow to rest for 15 minutes.

For the demi-glace:
Carmelize the sugar in a heavy saucepan. When sugar is a light brown color, carefully add the blackberries.

To prepare:

Saute the shallots in butter, adding dried fruit, port and spices. Reduce for two minutes, remove from heat and cool. In a mixing bowl, toss together the egg and bread and add into the fruit mixture. Reserve.

Take the pounded pork tenderloin and season with salt and pepper. Spoon the fruit mixture

Remove from heat and add the orange zest, orange juice and stock. Simmer for 30 minutes until reduced by half. Adjust seasoning with salt and pepper.

To serve: slice the tenderloin, plate and drizzle with the demi-glace. Serve with roasted potatoes and fresh vegetables.

142

Stuffed Pork Loin
With Cherry Zinfandel Sauce

Rolling Hills Country Club
Monroe, North Carolina

Larry Henfling Executive Chef
Serves 4-6

Ingredients:

1 pork loin roast, 4-6 pounds

For the brine:

¼ cup salt

½ cup brown sugar

46 ounces pineapple juice

For the stuffing:

1/3 cup dried mission figs, halved, sliced thin

1/3 cup dried apricots, julienne

1/3 cup sun-dried cherries, plumped

½ pound baby spinach

¼ cup toasted pine nuts

Bread crumbs

1 egg

Salt and pepper

For the sauce:

2 Tbls garlic, chopped

2 Tbls shallots

3 bay leaves

3 sprigs each, thyme and rosemary

8 whole black peppercorns

2 bottles zinfandel wine

2 cups sun-dried cherries

½ gallon demi glaze

½ cup brown sugar

Salt and pepper to taste

To prepare:

For the brine: Bring all the ingredients to a boil in a sauce pan, then cool in an ice bath until cold. Clean the pork loin and brine in the solution for 24 hours.

For the stuffing: blend all the ingredients together and refrigerate overnight while pork is brining.

For the sauce:

Place the garlic, shallots, bay leaf, rosemary, thyme, peppercorns and the zinfandel in a sauce pan and bring to boil. Reduce heat and simmer until it reduces by half. Add the demi glace and reduce by half again. Add the cherries and puree. Add the sugar and salt and pepper to taste.

Remove loin from brine. Butterfly cut the loin until it opens flat. Fill with the stuffing mix and roll closed. Truss with twine and place onto a sheet pan with an oven rack. Season with salt and pepper. Roast in a 350° oven until the pork reaches an internal temperature of 165°.

Let rest 10 minutes before removing truss. Serve slices of the roast pork drizzled with the warm sauce.

143

Wok Seared Mongolian Veal Chop
With Mushroom and Fava Bean Ragout and Tamarind Demi-Glaze

Orchid Island Golf & Beach Club
Vero Beach, Florida
Jeff McKinney, Executive Chef
Serves 4

Ingredients:

4-10 oz veal chops
For the marinade:
3 cloves garlic, finely chopped
1 Tbls minced ginger
1 Tbls minced shallot
¼ cup cilantro coarsely chopped
½ cup sherry vinegar
3 Tbls hoisin sauce
2 Tbls soy sauce
2 Tbls rice wine vinegar
1 Tbls sesame oil
2 Tbls smooth peanut butter
1 Tbls honey
2 Tbls hot chili sauce
For the Mushroom and Fava Beans Ragout:
2 cups dice portabella mushroom
2 cups fresh fava beans
1 cup tomato concasse (peeled, seeded, coarsely chopped)
2 tsp minced garlic
1 Tbls minced shallot
3 Tbls demi glaze
2 Tbls chopped parsley
Salt and pepper to taste
For the Tamarind demi-glaze
1 cup demi glaze
½ cup red wine
1 tsp tamarind paste (found in Asian mkts)
1 tsp minced shallots
½ tsp whole black pepper
1 tsp honey

To prepare:

Combine all marinade ingredients in shallow baking dish. Add veal chops to the mixture and turn to coat. Cover and let marinate 3 to 4 hours or overnight.

Heat 3 Tbls oil in the wok until it's nearly smoking. Remove veal from marinade and sear the chop for 7 to 8 minutes on each side or until cooked through.

For the Mushroom and Fava Beans Ragout:
Sautee the garlic and shallot for a couple of minutes.

Add mushroom, fava beans, tomato, demi glaze and parsley. Cook for another 4 to 5 minutes. Season with salt and pepper.

For the Tamarind demi-glaze
Put all the ingredients in a sauce pot. Heat and reduce to ¾ cup.

Strain the sauce and serve over veal chop with the ragout on the side.

144

Pasta, Poultry & More

Conecuh Smoked Sausage & Shrimp Pasta

Grand Hotel Marriott Resort
Point Clear, Alabama

Mike Wallace, Executive Chef

Serves 2

Ingredients:

4 ounces sliced Conecuh smoked sausage

1 Tbls butter

2 tsp chopped garlic

¼ cup leeks julienned

1 cup button mush rooms

1 red pepper julienne

8 16/20-count shrimp, peeled and deveined

1 Tbls Creole seasoning

1 bottle Abita or dark beer

8 ounces heavy cream

1 ½ tomatoes, diced

8 ounces angel hair pasta, cooked and oiled

¼ cup grated Parmesan cheese

To prepare:

Place sliced smoked sausage on a sheet pan and roast in a 400° oven until browned.

Remove from pan and place on paper towel.

Sauté garlic in butter until lightly browned. Add leeks, mushrooms, shrimp and red peppers and cook until tender.

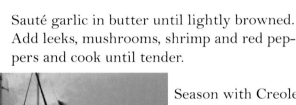

Season with Creole spice and deglaze with beer. Reduce by half, add cream, tomato and sausage.

Cook on medium heat until slightly thickened. Add cheese.

Heat pasta in boiling salted water until heated through, strain and mix with the sauce. Serve topped with additional Parmesan cheese.

Notes: Conecuh smoked sausage and Abita beer are local brands used at the hotel. You may substitute local products.

145

Gemelli Pasta
With Smoked Chicken Breast, Wild Mushrooms, Cherry Tomatoes and Asiago Sauce

Ingredients:

1 pound gemelli pasta
1 gallon water
3 Tbls salt
½ pound smoked chicken breast (Julienne)
1 cup button mushrooms cut in quarters
1 Tbls small diced yellow onion
1 tsp minced garlic
2 Tbls olive oil
½ cup shredded Asiago cheese
3 Tbls Chardonnay
2 ½ cups heavy whipping cream
8 cherry tomatoes, halved
2 Tbls Italian parlsey, chopped
Salt and pepper to taste

To prepare:

In a large pot, bring 1 gallon of water and 3 Tbls of salt to a boil. Cook the Gemelli pasta as recommended on the box. Once the pasta is cooked, strain and reserve warm.

In a large sauce pot, sauté the garlic, onions, mushrooms and the smoked chicken breast julienne in the olive oil for approximately 5 minutes or until the onions are translucent.

Deglaze with the Chardonnay and cook until the wine is dissolved but no browning is showing on the bottom of the pan.

Add the heavy whipping cream and bring to a

The Ritz-Carlton Lodge
Reynolds Plantation, Georgia

Scott C. Gambone, Executive Chef

Serves 4

boil allowing it to boil for approximately 2-4 minutes.

Add warm pasta to the sauce and toss in the chopped parsley, Asiago cheese and the cherry tomatoes. Season to taste.

Grown-Up Mac 'N' Cheese

Country Club of Columbus
Columbus, Georgia

John Weatherford, Executive Chef
Serves 4

Ingredients:

4 oz diced bacon
4 oz diced red onion
12 oz cream
4 oz shredded Parmesan cheese
4 oz goat cheese
5 oz American cheese
4 cups cooked penne pasta
Cracked black pepper
Salt
¼ cup seasoned bread crumbs

To prepare:

Render the bacon and cook the red onions in the grease, add the cream and bring to a simmer, add American, goat and parmesan cheese.

Add cooked penne pasta, cracked black pepper and salt to taste, place in a casserole dish and top with seasoned bread crumbs cook under broiler until golden brown.

Frog Legs
With Mango Rum Glaze

Rosen Shingle Creek Resort
Orlando, Florida
James R. Slattery, Executive Chef

Serves 4

Ingredients:
6 frog legs
1 cup buttermilk
2 Tbls Creole spice
Flour

For the Mango Rum Glaze:
1 cup fresh mango
¼ cup brown sugar
¼ cup cidar vinegar
¼ cup yellow onion, diced
1 lime, seeded
1 Tbls ginger root, grated
1 orange, seeded
2 Tbls molasses
1 lemon, seeded
1 clove garlic, minced
1 tsp mustard seed
¼ Tbls red pepper flakes
¼ Tbls ground cinnamon
¼ Tbls ground cloves
¼ Tbls allspice

2 Tbls chopped fresh cilantro
¼ cup dark rum

To prepare:
Cut frog legs in half, wash in cold water and marinate in buttermilk for 30 minutes.

Season the flour with salt and Creole spice.

Roll legs in flour mixture and fry in deep fat at 390° for 2-3 minutes until golden.

For the Mango Rum Glaze:
Combine all ingredients together except cilantro and rum. Cook over low heat for approximately 30 minutes. Remove from heat and puree. Return to heat and add the rum. Cook for five minutes, constantly stirring. Add cilantro and cool. Blend one more time until smooth.

To plate:
Place frog legs on platter with wilted spinach and drizzle with the mango rum glaze.

148

Seared Chicken Breast
With Anna Potatoes, Asparagus and Carmelized Mango Relish

Haig Point Club
Daufuskie Island, South Carolina
Gerard Brunett, Executive Chef
Serves 4

Ingredients:

4 chicken breasts, bone-in

For the mango relish:

1 mango peeled and pitted
1 tsp diced red pepper
1 tsp diced red onion
Minced cilantro (to taste)
1 tsp honey
Salt and pepper (to taste)
Olive oil

For the Anna potatoes:

3 Idaho potatoes, peeled and sliced thinly.
Olive oil

Salt and pepper

To prepare:

For the mango relish:
In a skillet heat a little oil. Place the mangos in the pan and sear until golden brown. Let cool and dice. In a stainless bowl combine remaining ingredients and let chill.

For the Anna potatoes:
Heat the oil in a non-stick pan over medium heat. Shingle the potato slices two layers deep. Season with salt & pepper and saute until golden brown and flip, cooking the other side as well. Remove from the pan, pat excess oil with paper towel and set aside.

Season chicken breasts with salt and pepper and sear until golden brown, finish in a 350° oven.

To plate:
Re-heat the potatoes in the oven. On a warm dinner plate place the potatoes in the middle and top with the chicken breast. Top the chicken off with equal parts of the relish. Place hot blanched asparagus against the chicken & serve.

Garnish with fresh herb sprig.

149

Sand Crane and Armadillo Stew

The Concession Golf Club
Bradenton, Florida

Sean Murphy, Culinary Director
Serves 6

Ingredients:

Kosher salt

Ground pepper

1 Tbls rosemary, crushed and finely chopped

½ Tbls sage

1 Tbls basil

Roasted duckling – deboned and skinned c cut into larger, thumb – sized chunks

2 handfuls Cipolini onions

1 handful each baby bliss potatoes and baby carrots

1 handful roasted parsnips cooked separately and cut finger sized. (parsnips can be overpowering if cooked in the stew so add them later or omit)

1 cup sherry

Roux – classic butter- flour roux

1 whole chicken, sectioned, breast cut in thirds across the bone

1-2 cups veal or chicken stock depending how rich and dark you want to make the stew. Veal stock or veal demi-glace (will add significant richness – use to taste.)

To prepare:

For the duckling:

Any standard method for roasting duckling will do. I recommend Maple Leaf Duckling as an excellent quality brand.

Debone the duckling, and deglazing the pan with port, saving the juices overnight in the refrigerator and then skimming and spooning off the congealed fat. Save some of the fat for searing the chicken and veggies.

This recipe was inspired by Jimmy Wright, a charming southern gentleman of impeccable manners and The Concession's Director of Golf. Showing me around the course for the first time, Jimmy's usual calm demeanor was upset only by seeing the damage done to his greens by the local armadillos and sand cranes. Although I understood that Jimmy would like us to use to real thing, this stew is actually make with chicken and roast duck!

--Sean Murphy

150

Save the skin of the duckling from the breast. Roast it extra crisp in the oven. Julienne it and keep for garnish on the stew.

For the stew:
Add a tablespoon of the duck fat to a relatively hot, large roasting pan on top of the stove. Season the chicken pieces with salt and pepper, dust with flour and sear to golden brown in a large braising pan. Add onions and carrots and brown evenly, reducing heat and adding a touch more duck fat as necessary.

When chicken, onions and carrots are nicely browned add the sherry, white wine and port. Reduce heat and simmer until the liquid is reduced by about half.

Add duckling pieces and duck pan juices. Add chicken or veal stock and potatoes. Simmer very slowly until potatoes are just cooked but still firm.

Thicken to desired consistency with roux. Add a couple of spoonfuls of butter to send it over the top.

Stir in parsnips. When parsnips are hot through ladle into in large serving bowls peasant style. Garnish with fresh rosemary and warmed, julienned duckling skin.

Serve with sides of mixed wild and brown rice laced with diced dried cranberries that can be spooned into the stew and a chunk of toasted brown bread.

A rich chardonnay like Mer and Soliel may stand with this dish but I would prefer a lusher Pinot Noir like the great one from Sonoma Coast Wineries or a lighter fruitier Cab like Alexander Valley Cabernet.

Wild Mushroom Ravioli

Gasparilla Inn & Club
Boca Grande, Florida
James Dyer, Executive Chef

Serves 4

Ingredients:

3 Tbls butter
1 red onion, minced
¾ cup marjoram or oregano, chopped fine
6 ounces dried porcini mushrooms, reconstituted
Olive oil as needed
4 cloves garlic, minced
1 ½ pound button mushrooms, sliced
3 pounds ricotta cheese, drained
8 ounces Parmesan cheese, grated fine
Nutmeg to taste
Fresh pasta dough

To prepare:

Sweat onion in butter over low heat until soft. Add marjoram. Stir to combine, season and chill.

Drain the porcinis, reserving the liquid. Rinse and hold. Sweat garlic in a little olive oil until fragrant. Add mushrooms, turn up the heat and sauté over high heat for 5 minutes. Add the porcini and turn the heat down to low. Cook over low heat for 20 minutes, moistening the mushrooms with the reserved porcini liquid; keep moist, not wet. Season and cool; chop roughly.

Mix onions, ricotta and parmesan together in a bowl. Season to taste with salt and pepper and nutmeg.

To assemble: roll out 6" wide pasta sheet. Lay down piles of filling about 2" apart running down the length of the pasta. Egg wash and fold pasta sheet over the filling, sealing in the filling. Cut the raviolis. Repeat until filling is gone. Toss with corn meal to keep separate.

When ready, boil 6-8 minutes, serve with a red sauce.

Seafood Dishes
Baked Yellowtail Snapper

The Naples Beach Hotel & Golf Club
Naples, Florida

Marwan Kassem, Executive Chef

Serves 2

Ingredients:

1 whole yellow tail snapper (1-1 ½ pounds)
2 ½ ounces lump crab meat
3 ounces heavy whipping cream
1/4 cup chopped fresh basil
½ cup diced shallots
1 ounce diced red &green bell pepper
1 ½ Tbls extra virgin olive oil

Salt and pepper to taste

To prepare:

Butterfly the fish and remove the head and the bone skelton, Keep the fillets attached to the tail.

Season the fish with salt, pepper and basil and sear on both sides in a hot skillet in the olive oil. Remove from pan and cool.

Saute shallots, diced peppers, and lump crab meat for 2 minutes in the oil.

Add heavy cream to the mixture and cook for 7 to 9 minutes. Remove from heat and cool.

Layer the crab mixture inside the fish.

Bake the fish in a pre-heated oven at 375° for 10 to 12 minutes. Place the fish on a plate and garnish with lemon and herbs.

© The Naples Beach Hotel & Golf Club

153

Bamboo Steamed Red Snapper
With Garlic Green Beans, Grilled Sweet Potatoes and Chive Ginger Beure Blanc

Orchid Island Golf & Beach Club
Vero Beach, Florida

Jeff McKinney, Executive Chef
Serves 4

Ingredients:

For the fish:

4 - 6 oz red snapper filets
1 tsp lemon zest
2 tsp minced garlic
15 each French green beans
10 – ¼ inch thick sliced sweet potatoes
1 Tbls peanut oil
1 oz chive ginger beure blanc (recipe below)

For the Chive Ginger Beure Blanc:

1 cup white wine
1 Tbls grated fresh Ginger
1 Tbls lemon juice
1 tsp minced shallots
1 Tbls minced fresh chive
¼ cup heavy cream
12 Tbls (1.5 sticks) unsalted butter (cut in pieces)

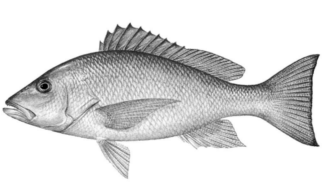

To prepare:

For the Chive Ginger Beure Blanc:

Reduce the white wine, ginger, lemon juice, shallot and chives to ¼ cup. Add the heavy cream and reduce by half. Stir in the butter by pieces.

Strain the sauce and keep warm.

For the fish:

Season the fish with salt, pepper and lemon zest, and then steam in a Chinese bamboo steamer about 6 to 7 minutes.

While waiting for the fish to cook, sauté the garlic in the oil till golden brown. Add the French green beans and cook until tender. Season the sweet potatoes with salt, pepper and peanut oil. Grill both sides about 3 minutes on each side.

Plate Presentation:

On the center of the plate, overlap the slices of sweet potatoes to make a round shape.

Put the garlic green beans on top of the potatoes. Add the red snapper filets on top. Ladle the sauce on top of the fish and around the edge of the plates.

154

Cedar Plank Wild Salmon
With Citrus Crust, Field Slaw &
Pear and Apple Chutney

Daniel Island Club
Charleston, South Carolina
Tyler M. Dudley, Executive Chef
Serves 4

Ingredients:

For the Salmon:
4 6-ounce portions of wild-caught salmon
   (skin removed)
1 tsp lemon zest
1 tsp lime zest
1 tsp orange zest
1 cup fresh bread crumbs
4 Tbls melted butter
1 Tbls minced shallot
Salt and pepper to taste
1 tsp brown sugar
For the Field Slaw:
1 jicama julienne
1 carrot julienne
1 daikon julienne
1 red pepper julienne
2 scallions thin sliced
¼ cup chopped cilantro
For the Slaw Dressing
1 cup mayonnaise
¼ cup grain mustard
2 Tblss cider vinegar
1/2 tsp celery salt
1 jucied lemon
1 pinch sugar
For the Pear and apple chutney
2 Bartlett pears peeled and chopped
2 Granny Smith apples peeled and chopped
1 cup golden raisins
½ cup sherry wine vinegar
½ cup sugar
½ tsp ground cinnamon

To prepare:

For the Field Slaw:
Combine all slaw dressing ingredients in a mixing bowl. Add field slaw ingredients, mix and adjust seasoning.

For the Pear and apple chutney:
Combine all ingredients in sauce pan and bring to a simmer. Cover and simmer for thirty minutes. Cool to room temperature before serving.

For the Salmon:
Soak a 15"-17" untreated cedar plank in water for a least 1 hour. Blanch zest and dry. Combine zest with bread crumbs, butter, shallots, salt and pepper, and sugar. Mix well.

Top each portion of salmon evenly with bread crumb mixture. Roast salmon on cedar planks in preheated 400° oven for 15 minutes.

To serve:
Place field slaw in the center of four plates, top with salmon and serve with side of chutney.

155

Cedar Plank Grilled Salmon With Baby Arugula and Waldorf Salad

Ingredients:

For the dry rub:
Makes about ¼ cup dry rub
2 tsp freshly grated pepper
1 tsp, grated lemon peel
1 tsp granulated garlic
1 tsp dried tarragon
1 tsp dried basil
1 Tbls paprika
1 Tbls sea salt
2 tsp light brown sugar

For the salmon:
1 cedar BBQ grilling plank
2 six-ounce pieces of salmon wild king fillet, about 2 inches thick, block cut
1 Tbls dry rub seasoning
1 lemon, cut into 4 wedges

For the Waldorf salad:
2/3 cup dried tart cherries (if available use fresh cherries--don't boil)
1 cup boiling water
½ cup mayonnaise
3 Tblss sour cream
2 Tblss fresh lemon juice
1 tsp sugar
4 Granny Smith apples, cored, cut into cubes
1 1/3 cups very thinly sliced celery
1 1/3 cups red seedless grapes, halved

For the Arugula salad:
1 cup baby organic arugula
4 Tblss Cilantro Key Lime Vinaigrette

Marietta Country Club Kennesaw, Georgia

Sean McLendon, Executive Chef
Serves 2

For the vinaigrette:
½ bunch cilantro, cleaned
¼ onion, peeled and diced large
2 cloves garlic
1 can chipolte peppers
2 cups red wine vinegar
1 cup lime juice
½ cup egg yolks, pasteurized
¼ can hoison sauce
4 cups grape seed oil
1 cup water
Juice of 2 limes
Salt

To prepare:

For the dry rub:
Place dry rub ingredients in a food processor or spice grinder and process until well blended. Transfer to a small bowl or cup, wrap tightly and store at room temperature until ready to use.

For the salmon:
Soak the cedar plank for at least 5 hours. Place the fillets on wax paper. Sprinkle both sides of the fish evenly with the dry rub (1 ½ tsp per serving). Press the seasoning into the flesh. Refrigerate the salmon, uncovered, for at least 2 hours and up to 12 hours.

Place the salmon pieces in the center of the cedar plank. Squeeze a lemon wedge over the covered with gray ash. Cover with a lid.

For the Waldorf salad:
Soak cherries in 1 cup boiling water until softened, about 10 minutes. Drain.

Whisk mayonnaise and next 3 ingredients
in large bowl. Add apples, celery, grapes and
cherries; toss. Season with salt and pepper.

For the vinaigrette:
Blend the cilantro, onion, garlic, chipotle, vinegar, lime juice and yolks.

Add the hoison sauce and blend. Emulsify in
the blend oil. Temper in the water to adjust
consistency. Squeeze in the fresh lime juice.
Season with salt and pepper.

Serve as shown below.

Chive Roasted Spot-Tail Bass
With White Truffle Risotto

Long Cove Club
Hilton Head Island, South Carolina
Leonard Giarratano, Executive Chef
Serves 2

Ingredients:

For the Bass:
2 fillets spot-tailed bass (also called redfish
   or red drum)
½ cup fresh chopped chives
1 tsp paprika
2 Tbls ground Saltine crackers
2 tsp Kosher salt
¼ tsp Cayenne pepper
1/3 cup extra-virgin olive oil

For the Risotto:
8 cups chicken broth, heated
2 Tbls extra-virgin olive oil
1 yellow onion, finely chopped
1 large garlic clove, minced
2 cups Arborio rice
¼ cup dry white wine
½ cup grated Asiago cheese
1 cup fresh arugula
3 Tbls white truffle oil
Salt and freshly ground pepper, to taste
½ cup sugar
½ tsp ground cinnamon

To prepare:
Pre-heat oven to 400°.

For the bass:
Mix together the oil, the paprika, salt, Cayenne pepper, and chives in a mixing bowl.

Dip fillets in this mixture and place on a non-stick baking pan. Set aside and start the risotto.

For the risotto:
In a non-stick sauce pan over medium-high heat, warm the olive oil. Add the onions and cook until the onions become slightly soft, about 2-3 minutes. Add the garlic and cook 1 minute more.

Add the rice and stir with a wooden spoon. Cook, while stirring, about 3 minutes. Add the wine and stir frequently until absorbed. Turn heat down to medium and begin adding broth one ladle-full at a time, stirring until it is almost completely absorbed before adding the next.

When half the broth is remaining, place the fish in the oven. The fish will need to cook about 12-15 minutes.

When the rice is tender, add the arugula and cook one more minute.

Remove from heat, stir in the Asiago, truffle oil, salt and pepper.

Serve fish atop the risotto.

158

Cumin Crusted Halibut
With Warm Soba Noodle Salad and Poblano Vinaigrette

Northwood Country Club
Meridian, Mississippi

Jake Clara, Executive Chef
Serves 4

Ingredients:

For the halibut:
4 6-8 oz. halibut filets
5 Tbsp ground cumin
3 Tbsp olive oil

For the poblano vinaigrette:
¼ cup rice vinegar
¾ cup extra virgin olive oil
1 Tbsp Dijon mustard
1 Tbsp honey
1/2 tsp salt
1 poblano pepper, small dice
1 red bell pepper, small dice
1 bunch cilantro, minced
½ bunch Italian parsley leaves, stemmed, washed and minced
8 sprigs fresh thyme leaves, stripped and minced
1 cup Madeira wine

For the warm soba noodle salad:
1 **package soba noodles** (*soba noodles may be purchased at local Asian markets or in grocery stores with a specialty area*)
1 cup
1 quart water

2 Tbls salt

To prepare:

For the halibut:
Preheat oven to 350°
Spread cumin in an even layer on a plate or pie dish. Lay each halibut filet (presentation side down) in cumin and press firmly to create an even crust.

Heat olive oil in a medium size sauté pan (medium-high heat). Shake off excess cumin and lay halibut filets (cumin side down) in olive oil.
Sauté until cumin is golden brown then flip and finish in 350 degree oven. (8-10 minutes).

For the poblano vinaigrette:
Combine vinegar, Dijon mustard, honey, and salt in a food processor or medium size mixing bowl. Pulse or whisk to combine well.

To serve: Toss cooked soba noodles with vinaigrette and place in center of plate. Place a halibut filet on top, Garnish with lemon wedges.

159

Florida Golden Tile Soubise
With Cococut Jasmine Rice and Roasted Beets

Grand Harbor
Vero Beach, Florida
Andrew Carmack, Executive Chef
Serves 4

Ingredients:

For the Golden Tile:
4-8 oz. filets Florida Golden Tile (a firm white-flesh fish. Can substitute amberjack, tilapia, grouper, or snapper)
2 large Vidalia onions
1 clove garlic
3 cups white wine
2 cups heavy cream
1 large lemon, for juice & zest
Bread crumbs as needed

For the Coconut Jasmine rice:
3 cups Jasmine rice
3 cups chicken stock
2 cups coconut milk
2 cups shredded coconut, toasted
½ cup chives
Salt and pepper

For the roasted beets:
2 pounds fresh beets
¼ cup olive oil
1 large garlic clove
¼ tsp thyme

To prepare:

For the Golden Tile:
Peel and quarter onions and place in a sauce pan. Add garlic, white wine and heavy cream. Simmer for 20 minutes (or until mixture becomes thick).

Place mixture in food processor and blend. It will turn into butter. Season with salt & pepper. Add chopped lemon zest and lemon juice. Season fish fillets with salt and pepper. Spread mixture over fillets. Sprinkle with bread crumbs. Bake for 15 minutes at 350°. Serve

For the Coconut Jasmine rice:
Rinse rice twice with cold water. Add chicken stock, coconut milk and salt & pepper. Mix together.

Place in a sauce pan and bring to boil, then turn down heat and simmer. Cook for 20 minutes or until liquid has evaporated. Cover pot with lid and let steam for 5 minutes.

Remove lid, fluff rice with serving fork, fold in toasted coconut and chives.

For the roasted beets:
Boil beets in pot of water until tender, about 20 minutes. Chill until cold. Peel beets and slice into wedges. Toss beets with garlic, thyme, salt & pepper. Roast for 5 minutes at 350°.

Serve fish on bed of rice with beets on side.

160

Georgia Brook Trout
With Peach Salsa and Sweet Potatoes

Ingredients:

For the trout:

8 fresh brook trout, scaled, boned and butterfly cut, about 10 oz each

4 large eggs, whisked smooth

½ cup Canola oil

½ cup all-purpose flour

For the Pecan Crust:

3 cups pecan pieces, (about the size of rice)

4 Tbls fresh oregano, chopped fine

2 Tbls fresh basil, chopped fine

2 Tbls fresh chives, chopped fine

1 cup all-purpose flour

For the Peach Salsa Fresca:

1 pound peaches, pitted and cut into quarter-inch cubes (can use frozen)

Juice from 3 limes

4 plum tomatoes cut into 1/4-inch cubes

1 bunch green onions, sliced (both green and white sections)

1 Jalapeno pepper, chopped fine with seeds (remove seeds for less spicy version)

1 Tbls cilantro leaves, chopped

¼ cup extra virgin olive oil

¼ cup sherry wine vinegar

¼ cup honey

Kosher salt and white pepper to taste

For the Grilled Sweet Potatoes

2 sweet potatoes, large

2 Tbls olive oil

1 Tbls fresh thyme leaves, chopped

Salt and black pepper to taste

To prepare:

For the Peach Salsa Fresca:

Reynolds Plantation Resort
Lake Oconee, Georgia

Gerald Schmidt, Executive Chef

Serves 8

Combine all ingredients in a stainless steel mixing bowl. Season with salt and white pepper to taste. Refrigerate.

For the Grilled Sweet Potatoes

Pierce potatoes with the tip of a paring knife about 5 times each. Place in a pre-heated 325° oven. Roast for about 40 minutes or until there is no resistance when you pierce with a knife, remove to cool down. Remove skin; slice the peeled sweet potato in 1/2" slices. Brush with oil, sprinkle with thyme, salt and pepper. Place on hot grill, achieving grill marks on both sides of potato. Remove and keep warm.

For the Pecan Crust:

In a mixing bowl, combine all the ingredients thoroughly. Cover and reserve for crusting.

For the trout:

Dredge trout through seasoned flour, then in the egg wash and finally in the pecan crust preparation. Place 1/4 of the oil in a large non-stick fry pan over medium high heat. Place trout skin side up, toward you. Cook until pecans turn golden brown, then turn over and repeat (about 3-4 minutes per side.) Once both sides are cooked, remove from pan and keep warm. Repeat until all trout are cooked.

To plate: Place cooked fish on platter. Top with salsa and equally distribute the grilled sweet potatoes on the side of the fish.

Fennel-Crusted Halibut
With Cheese & Squash Risotto and Berry Sauce

Ingredients:

For the Halibut:

4 - 6 oz. baby halibut fillet skin on, seasoned with the fennel seasoning (see below)

Vegetable oil for searing

For the fennel seasoning:

2 tsp fennel, lightly toasted and coarsely ground

8 tsp sea salt

Combine all the above and mix well

For the Sauce:

6 oz. dried berries (your choice)

1 cup pomegranate juice

1 cup Gewürztraminer wine

¼ pound (1 stick) butter cubed

Salt and pepper to taste

For the Risotto:

3 Tbls olive oil

4 tsp butter

½ large onion, fine diced

¼ cup white wine (Gewürztraminer)

¼ cup butternut squash, peeled, seeded, cubed

1 cup Arborio rice

½ cup grated Parmigiano-Reggiano

2 oz. goat cheese

5-8 cups vegetable stock, warmed to simmer

Ginn Reunion Resort Orlando, Florida

Christian Schmidt, Executive Chef

Serves 4

To prepare:

For the risotto:

Sautee squash in a pan with a little butter until golden brown. Season with salt and pepper and keep warm.

Heat stock to slowly simmering in a separate sauce pan. Heat a large, heavy skillet over medium heat. Add olive oil and ½ the butter.

When butter is just melted, add onions (don't brown), stir to coat and sauté for 5 minutes.

Add Arborio rice, stir to coat well Add wine and allow to be absorbed. Make sure it is room temperature or it will harden the rice. Reduce heat to low and add just enough warm stock to cover the rice. As rice is uncovered, keep adding warm stock as needed to just cover the rice. Continue this process for about 20 minutes, stirring constantly with a wooden spoon, until rice is tender.

When the last stock added has reduced to about 90 percent abosrbed, add remaining butter. Stir in well, then add Parmigiano-Reggiano and the goat cheese and stir it in well.

Add the warm squash and mix in gently.

Remove from heat and let rest for 5 minutes while final liquid is absorbed. The risotto should be rich and creamy. Rice should be tender.

For the Sauce:
Combine dried berries, pomegranate juice, and wine and reduce by 2/3 slowly. Remove from heat. Incorporate the butter with whisk. Strain and set aside and hold at 100°.

For the Halibut:
Pan sear skin-side down in medium hot non-stick pan until skin is crispy. Sear on all sides until medium well (145°).

Remove and rest for 2-3 minutes then serve immediately.

To serve:
Spoon risotto onto plate, and top with halibut fillet. Drizzle with sauce and serve.

Ginger Snap Crusted Grouper
With Mango-Citrus Sauce and Polenta Cakes

Ingredients:
4 8-ounce filets of Grouper, bones removed
3 cups ginger snap coating (below)
Mango-citrus sauce (below)
Polenta Cakes (below)

For the Ginger Snaps coating:
3 ¾ cups flour
3 tsp baking soda
2 tsp ground ginger
1 tsp ground cinnamon
1 tsp cloves
12 Tbls (1 ½ sticks) unsalted butter, softened
2 cups brown sugar, packed
2 eggs, beaten
½ cup molasses
2 tsp lime juice
1 tsp vanilla

For the Mango-Citrus Sauce:
4 mangos, ripe
3 Tbls butter
3 Tbls brown sugar
¼ cup orange juice, fresh
¼ mango puree
2 Tbls spiced rum

For the Polenta Cakes:
2 tsps onions, diced
2 Tbls unsalted butter
1 quart chicken stock
6 ounces polenta
Salt and pepper to taste

To prepare:
Cookies: Sift together flour, baking soda, ginger, cinnamon and cloves. In a mixer, cream

Croasdaile Country Club
Durham, North Carolina
Tim Gauldin, Executive Chef

together butter and brown sugar. Add the beaten eggs. Add to butter mixture the molasses, lime juice and the vanilla. Gradually add flour and mix as little as possible to combine. Divide mixture and wrap in plastic. Allow to rest in refrigerator for at least one hour. Pat cookies into 3 inch diameters and place on parchment lined cookie sheet. Bake at 350 degrees for about 10 minutes. Remove from oven and allow cooling completely until crisp. They will still be extremely soft when removed from oven. Once cool and crisp grind in food processor by pulsing.

Fish: Coat each grouper fillet with ground ginger snaps. Place on a greased cookie sheet and bake in a 350° oven for approximately 20 to 25 minutes.

Polenta Cakes: Sauté onions in butter for one minute. Then add stock and bring to a boil. Slowly add polenta whisking constantly to prevent lumps. Adjust seasoning with salt and pepper and simmer for 30 minutes. Scrape polenta into a 9 ½ by 11 greased pan and spread evenly. Chill till set. Cut polenta into desired shapes i.e. Cylinders or triangles. Broil in oven for 5 to 7 minutes.

To *plate:* Arrange each filet on plate with several polenta pieces. Drizzle sauce on top and serve.

Grilled Red Snapper
With Pad Thai Noodles

Hendersonville Country Club
Hendersonville, North Carolina

Steve Greenhoe, Executive Chef

Serves 4

Ingredients:

8 ounces pad thai (rice stick noodles)
1 Tbls salad oil
4 six-ounce portions of red snapper fillets
½ cup fresh spinach
¼ cup carrots, cut into match sticks
¼ cup green bell pepper strips
¼ cup red bell pepper strips

For the dipping sauce:
2 tsps garlic, chopped
¼ Tbls red chili paste
   (optional)
1 ½ tsps minced ginger
   root
1 ½ tsps cilantro, chopped
3 ounces soy sauce
3 Tbls lime juice
2 ounces water
2 Tbls brown sugar
4 tsp toasted sesame oil

Prepare carrots and peppers and set aside. Combine the ingredients for the dipping sauce and set aside.

Grill the snapper fillets taking care not to overcook.

Saute carrots and bell peppers until tender in a small amount of oil. Add spinach leaves and stir until cooked. Add noodles and half of the dipping sauce and stir gently until the noodles are hot.

Remove noodles from heat and place in the center of each plate. Place a grilled snapper fillet, skin side up, over the noodes. Serve immediately with remainder of the dipping sauce.

To prepare:

Soak pad thai noodles in cold water for 30 minutes. Drain noodles and place in boiling water for 3-4 minutes, then drain and cool with cold water and set aside.

Remove any remaining scales from snapper fillets and cut two diagonal strips in the skin to reduce curling on the grill. Lightly oil the fillets with salad oil.

165

Grilled Tuna
With Andouille-Tortilla Chiaquiles, Guacamole and Charred Tomato Salsa

Camp Creek Golf Club
WaterSound, Florida

Bryan Ross, Executive Chef
Serves 4

Ingredients:

For the tuna and chiaquiles
4 tuna steaks (5-6 ounces each)
½ cup Andouille sausage, chopped
½ cup scallions, sliced thin
1 Tbls garlic, chopped
1 cup chicken broth
½ cup cheddar cheese, shredded
3 cups tortilla chips
Creole seasoning, to taste

For the Guacamole:
3 ripe avocados
1 Jalapeno, seeds removed and minced fine
¼ cup cilantro, chopped
½ cup red onion, diced
3 limes, juiced
Salt and pepper to taste

For Charred Tomato Salsa:
5-6 ripe Roma tomatoes, whole
2 Jalapeno peppers, whole, stem removed
1 small red onion, peeled, cut into rings
1 Tbls olive oil
½ bunch cilantro
4-5 limes, juiced
Salt and black pepper, to taste

To prepare:

In a medium non-stick skillet, saute the sausage, scallions and garlic until the sausage begins to release some of its fat. Add the chicken broth and cheddar cheese, and heat until cheese has melted. Crush tortillas with your hands and add to the pan, mix well with a wooden spoon or spatula.

For the Guacamole:
In a non-reactive bowl, mash all ingredients together with a spoon or a potato masher. Adjust seasoning if you prefer more lime.

Guacamole is best if left, covered, in the refrigerator for about 1 hour (this allows the acid from the lime juice to break down and develop the jalapeno and cilantro flavors)

For Charred Tomato Salsa:
Toss the whole tomatoes, jalapenos and red onion rings with salt, pepper and olive oil. Lay all on the hottest part of a grill and char on all sides until tomatoes and jalapeno blister, and onions are crisp around the edges. Remove from grill. Place all into food processor and puree.

Season the tuna steaks with creole seasoning, and grill -- 4-5 minutes per side for well done.

Portion chilaquiles evenly onto four plates, top with grilled tuna, guacamole and salsa, Enjoy!

Lemon Ginger Salmon
With Wasabi Aioli & Fisherman's Rice
Benvenue Country Club
Rocky Mount, North Carolina

David Baudier, Executive Chef
Serves 4

Ingredients:
4 six-ounce salmon filets

For the Marinade:
1 cup vegetable oil
½ cup fresh ginger, fine dice
1 ½ cups soy sauce
1 ½ cups lemon juice
1 cup granulated sugar

For the Soy Ginger Glaze:
1 ounce fresh ginger, fine dice
8 ounces soy sauce
1 Tbls crushed red pepper
4 ounces lemon juice
Corn starch slurry

For the Wasabi Aioli:
1 cup mayonnaise
2 Tbls wasabi paste

For the Fisherman's Rice
1 ½ cup seafood stock
1 cup wild rice
½ yellow onion
4 ounces asparagus ends, sliced on bias
3 ounces diced salmon
1 ounce lump crab

To prepare:
Marinate the salmon in the marinade for approximately 3 hours. Heat a sauté pan with 1 ounce of clarified butter. Sear the flesh side of the salmon first and then flip.

Place the fish in an oven heated to 375° for 12 minutes. When salmon is cooked, baste with the soy-ginger glaze and place back in the oven for an addition 2 minutes.

For the Fisherman's rice:
Sauté the yellow onions in 1 ounce of clarified butter. Add seafood stock to deglaze the pan. When stock comes to a boil, add the rice, then place in a 350° oven for 15-20 minutes or until the rice has absorbed the stock.

To assemble dish:
Saute the asparagus, crabmeat and diced salmon until the salmon is tender. Add the rice and spoon onto plate. Place salmon on top of the rice and drizzle with the wasabi aioli.

Serving Ideas: Garnish with sesame seeds.

167

Pan Roasted Corvina
With Grilled Potato-Vegetable Salad and Smoked Shrimp Gazpacho

Primland Resort
Meadows of Dan, Virginia
Britt Saylor, Executive Chef
Serves 4

Ingredients:

4 6-ounce filets of corvina or your favorite fish (snapper, , grouper, mahi mahi etc.)

For the Smoked Shrimp Gazpacho:
3 vine ripe tomatoes
1 stalk celery
½ small sweet onion
1 cucumber (peeled & seeded) Save ½ & dice to fold in later
½ red bell pepper
2 garlic cloves chopped
2 Tbls red wine vinegar
¼ baguette, crust removed
¼ cup extra virgin olive oil
Salt and pepper to taste
½ bunch fresh flat leaf parsley
Tomato juice if needed
¼ pound smoked or grilled shrimp cooked & diced

For the Grilled Potato Salad:
1 Belgium endive quartered
1 radicchio quartered
½ red bell pepper, diced
2 ½ inch slices red onion
½ cup rough chopped spinach
¼ cup balsamic vinegar
¾ cup extra virgin olive oil

6 to 8 equal sized Yukon gold potatoes boiled al dente, cooled and sliced ½ inch thick)

To prepare:

For the Smoked Shrimp Gazpacho:
Pulse all ingredients but diced cucumber & shrimp in food processor or use a hand mixer to puree. Fold in diced cucumber & shrimp adding tomato juice if needed a little at a time. Chill & adjust seasoning.

For the *Grilled Potato Salad:*
Mix vinegar and oil mix together in a bowl, then add first four ingredients tossing to coat. Marinate for 1 hour.

Grill potatoes over medium heat turning once. When cooked add to bowl along with rough chopped spinach and toss, adding salt & pepper to taste.

Pan sear or grill the fish. Serve with bowl of gazpacho and the potato salad.

168

Pan Seared Grouper
With Shrimp & Scallop Cream Sauce

Bluewater Bay Resort
Niceville, Florida
Timothy Yeabower, Executive Chef
Serves 4

Ingredients:

4 grouper fillets
½ pound 40-50 count shrimp
½ pound bay scallops
1 cup flour
1 cup heavy cream
1 red pepper, diced
1 green onion, sliced
2 Tbls Chef Paul's blackened redfish
   seasoning
2 Tbls cornstarch slurry
1 pound roasted potatoes
½ pound green beans

In the same large pan saute the peppers and green onions along with the shrimp and scallops until almost done.

Add the heavy cream & the blackened redfish seasoning and bring the cream to a boil. Add the slurry to thicken the sauce.

Place some roasted potatoes on a plate & top with green beans.

Place the grouper on top of the stack & ladle the sauce over the grouper.

To prepare:

Dredge the grouper in flour & pan sear in a large pan with 1/2 cup oil. Sear both sides till golden & place in a baking dish. Bake in 350° oven for 5 to 8 minutes. Keep warm.

Pan-Roasted Striped Bass
With Truffled Polenta, 'Barigoule' Artichokes & Crunchy Asparagus Salad

San Jose Country Club
Jacksonville, Florida

Jean-Christophe Setin, Executive Chef
Serves 2

Ingredients:

2 4-ounce portions of fresh striped bass
2 large fresh artichokes
5 ounces Italian polenta
2 Tbls truffled butter
1 bunch of fresh asparagus
¼ cup creme fraiche
1 lemon
Salt, pepper
Olive oil
1 carrot
1 sprig of thyme
1 clove of garlic
1 cup white wine

To prepare:

Blanch the asparagus in boiling salted water until tender but not too soft. Cut them in half.

Season the striped bass. Clean the artichokes by removing all outer leaves and removing the feathery heart. Cut in quarters. Set aside in lemony water. Peel and chop the carrots in ¼ inch thick slices.

In a skillet, heat up olive oil and throw in the artichokes, thyme, garlic clove and carrots. Over high flame allow to get very hot by covering the pot. When the vegetables are "singing" real loud, deglaze with the white wine and cover again. Turn down heat and simmer for 5 minutes. Season with salt and pepper.

In a glass bowl, mix creme fraiche, 1/2 lemon's juice, salt, pepper, and asparagus. Set aside.

Cook the polenta and fold in the truffled butter. Set aside.

Heat up olive oil in a skillet and sear the fish skin side first and press with an offset spatula in order to crisp up the skin. Finish in oven for 3 minutes at 350°. Remove from oven and allow to set for 5 minutes.

On the plate, place a small dollop of polenta, surrounded by few quarters of artichokes. Place the fish and the asparagus salad on top. Use a little Balsamic reduction for design on the plate.

WINE SUGGESTION: Talbott, "Sleepy Hollow Vineyard", California.

Pecan Encrusted Grouper
With Confetti Rice, Peach Chutney and Peach Beurre Blanc

Grand Hotel Marriott Point Clear, Alabama

Mike Wallace, Executive Chef
Serves 10

Ingredients:

10 fresh grouper fillets, 7 ounces
1 cup pecan pieces
1 ½ cups panko bread crumbs
1 cup flour
1 cup egg wash

For the rice:
30 ounces wild rice, cooked
1 cup each trio
   peppers, red
   onions, carrots
   and celery

For the chutney:
30 ounces fresh
   peaches, medium
   diced
1 cup red onion,
   medium diced
1 cup trio peppers,
   medium diced
¾ cup brown sugar
1 Tbls ginger, minced
2 ounces peach schnapps
1 Tbls vanilla extract

For the peach beurre blanc:
1 ½ cups chopped peaches
¼ tsp shallots
1 bouquet garni
3 ounces peach schnapps
½ cup clam juice
½ cup apple juice

½ cup honey
1/4 pound (1 stick) butter
Corn starch to thicken

To prepare:

Crust the grouper fillets by dipping in egg wash, flour, panko bread crumbs and pecan pieces. Saute in heavy skillet in 2 Tbls olive oil. Set aside and keep warm.

For the rice: Saute vegetables and add into rice. Season as needed.

For the chutney: sauté peaches and vegetables with the ginger for 3-4 minutes. Add sugar and caramelize slightly. Deglaze with schnapps and vanilla and simmer for about 2-3 minutes.

For the beurre blanc: Sauté peaches and shallots. Deglaze with liquids, add bouquet garni. Reduce by a quarter, then add corn starch to thicken to sauce consistency. Puree and strain. Add butter by whisking into hot sauce thoroughly.

Plate grouper fillets with confetti rice and chutney and drizzle with beurre blanc.

Prosciutto-Wrapped Grouper
With Melon Salsa & Lime Basmati Pilaf

Ingredients:

For the Grouper:
4 4-6 oz. filets of grouper
4 pieces prosciutto (shaved very thin)
3 Tbls olive oil
Kosher salt & black pepper to taste

For the Lime basmati pilaf:
1 cup basmati rice
2 cups water
1 lime juice & zest
½ Tbls butter
¼ tsp salt
Black pepper to taste

For the melon salsa:
1 cup cantaloupe, peeled & seeded, dice
¼ cup cucumber, peeled & seeded, dice
1 Tbls cilantro, minced
2 Tbls jalapeno, seeded, small dice
2 Tbls shallot, minced
2 Tbls. extra virgin olive oil
2 Tbls rice vinegar
1 tsp granulated sugar
¼ tsp kosher salt
Black pepper to taste

To prepare:

For the Grouper:
Season grouper filets with salt and pepper to taste. Wrap 1 piece of prosciutto around the center of each filet and press firmly to make the prosciutto stick together. (the seam of the prosciutto should be on the bottom of the filet).

Northwood Country Club
Meridian, Mississippi
Jake Clara, Executive Chef
Serves 4

Heat olive oil to medium-high in a medium sized non-stick sauté pan. Carefully place grouper filets in olive oil and saute until prosciutto is crispy (about 3 minutes).

Flip and finish cooking in saute pan (if thin enough) or place in a 350° oven until cooked thoroughly (about 5 more minutes).

For the Lime basmati pilaf:
Bring water to boil in a medium size saucepan, add rice and bring back to a boil. Reduce heat to low, cover and simmer for 15-20 minutes (until water is absorbed).

Transfer rice to a medium mixing bowl and add lime juice and zest, butter, salt & pepper. Toss gently until butter is melted.

For the melon salsa:
Add all ingredients into a medium sized mixing bowl. Toss gently and let sit for at least 30 minutes.

To assemble:
Use a portion scoop or large spoon and place rice pilaf in the center of a dinner plate. Place grouper filet on top of rice pilaf, then place a generous amount of melon salsa on top of each grouper filet. Garnish with sliced jalapenos or citrus and serve.

172

Roast 'N' Toast

Woodlands Resort & Inn
Summerville, South Carolina

Tarver King, Executive Chef
Serves 2

Ingredients:
6 ounces white fish (swordfish, grouper, snapper etc.)

1 cup pine nuts
2 Tbls extra-virgin olive oil
3 cloves garlic, peeled and left whole
10 large green grapes (peeled)
Large knob of French butter
¾ cup Lucques olives (pitted)
1 Tbls rosemary (chopped fine)
3 Tbls leaf parsley (chopped fine)
Thin slice sourdough bread (one for each fish portion)
2 sprigs rosemary
Salt and white pepper to taste

For the olive vinaigrette:
I cup black olive brine
1 Tbls red white vinegar
½ tsp Dijon mustard
2 Tbls extra-virgin olive oil
1 Tbls lemon juice
1 Tbls minced black olives

To prepare:
Warm the olive oil and garlic in a sauté pan until the garlic becomes golden brown and smells fragrant. Add the olives and fry until they begin to wrinkle and barely color. Add the pine nuts and stir constantly until they become golden brown. Check the seasoning and add the chopped herbs. Spread the pine nut mixture out on paper towels to cool.

Bring the fish up to room temperature and season with salt and pepper. Let the fish rest on a plate. When the fish begins to "sweat" wrap each piece with a slice of sourdough. Melt the butter on medium high in an iron skillet or non-stick pan. When the butter becomes "foamy" add the wrapped fish and rosemary sprigs. Saute for about 3 minutes or until "toasty" brown. Flip the fish only once as it will become soggy if rolled around too much. Drain the fish on paper towels and keep warm (the longer the fish rests, the less crispy the final dish).

For the vinaigrette:
Mix all ingredients together and keep cold in a sealed container.

To plate:
Warm the olive mixture and add the grapes. Spoon onto the middle of a plate and place the crispy fish on top. Spoon some vinaigrette around the dish and serve.

Pepper Encrusted Trout
With Wild Mushroom Risotto and Creamed Ramps

High Hampton Inn & Country Club
Cashiers, North Carolina

Bob Scholler,, Executive Chef
Serves 4

Ingredients:

For the Trout
4 large trout filets
4 Tbls coarsely ground black pepper
Salt
1 ounce brandy (optional)
1 ounce chicken broth
Non-stick cooking spray

For the Wild Mushroom Risotto:
1½ cups arborio rice
1 medium onion, finely diced
1/4 pound (1 stick) of butter
4 ounces crimini mushrooms, sliced
4 ounces shitake mushrooms, stems removed and sliced
5 cups chicken broth
2 ounces white wine (optional)
½ cup fresh grated Parmesan cheese
Salt and fresh ground pepper

For the Creamed Ramps:
1¼ pounds or about 24 ramps (wild leeks)
4-6 ounces cream
Salt and fresh ground pepper

To prepare:

For the Trout:
Wash filets and pat dry with a paper towel. Lightly sprinkle with salt. Pour pepper onto a plate and lay filets (flesh side down) onto the pepper. Gently press the filet to make the pepper stick.

Heat a large skillet on high heat until it is smoking hot, then spray with non-stick cooking spray. Sear the trout pepper side down for 1 minute then flip. Cook another minute and a half and remove pan from heat.

Carefully splash pan with brandy and swirl. Return the pan to heat to cook off brandy, then add chicken broth.

Cook until the liquid has reduced by one half. Reserve and keep warm.

For the Wild Mushroom Risotto:
Using half of the butter, saute the onions over medium-low heat in a Dutch oven until slightly browned (about 7 minutes). Add mushrooms and stir until fragrant (about 2 minutes), then add the rice.

Stir until glossy and well coated with butter. Once the rice begins to smell toasted, add wine and stir until absorbed, then stir in 1 cup of the broth. Stir frequently until rice absorbs liquid, and then add another cup. Continue adding the broth until 1/2 cup remains.

At this point you should taste the rice to check for doneness. It should be done but not mushy. Stir in remaining butter and cheese. Salt and pepper to taste.

The remaining 1/2 cup of broth can be used in case the rice needs more liquid to finish cooking, or to cream the rice back up if it is to be served at a later time.

For the Creamed Ramps:
Preheat oven to 375°.

Trim the root ends of the ramps, being careful not to cut off too much of the white portion as this will cause them to fall apart. Trim off the greens and slice for garnish (like scallions).

Tightly arrange ramps in a baking dish in one layer and fill dish with cream halfway up the sides of the ramps. Generously season with salt and pepper. Place in the oven.

After 20 minutes, use a fork or spoon to push the ramps back into the cream as they will begin to curl up. Bake another 10-15 minutes (until the cream has thickened but has not turned oily).

To Serve:
Spoon risotto onto the center of four plates and place the trout on top. Spoon the ramps and cream over top and serve.

175

Potato and Basil Wrapped Grouper
With Roasted Asparagus Cream, Spinach and Roasted Pepper and Sweet Corn Stew

Ingredients:

For the Grouper:
4 4-6 ounce thin-cut grouper medallions
2 Tbls olive oil
1 Tbls butter
¼ cup mayonnaise
Juice of 1 lemon
Salt and pepper to taste
1 leaf fresh basil leaf, chopped
4-6 Yukon Gold potatoes, sliced paper-thin
 on mandoline

For the Asparagus sauce:
2 cups asparagus tips
2 shallots, chopped
2 cloves garlic
Salt & pepper
½ cup brandy
1 ½ cups chicken stock
1 cup heavy cream

For the stew:
1 Tbls olive oil
½ cup fresh corn, chopped
¼ cup roasted red pepper, julienne
1 tsp garlic, chopped
3 cups fresh spinach, chopped
1 tsp cumin powder
¼ cup heavy cream
1 Tbls sugar
Salt and pepper to taste

Emerald Greens Private Resort
Tampa, Florida
Kaz Siftar, Executive Chef
Serves 4

To Prepare:

For the Grouper:
Lightly flour the grouper medallions, season with salt and pepper and place in sauté pan over medium-high heat with the butter and 1 tablespoon olive oil. Allow grouper to brown, cooking about halfway done and remove from heat.

In a small mixing bowl, combine the mayonnaise, lemon juice and a pinch of salt and pepper. Rub the mayonnaise mixture on the fish and add the basil.

Blanch the potatoes and place on the grouper in overlapping layers.

In another frying pan heat another tablespoon of olive oil on high heat and sauté the potato-wrapped fish until brown and crispy on both sides. Season with salt and pepper.

For the Asparagus cream sauce:
Add the asparagus tips, shallots, garlic and salt and pepper to a sauce pan and allow

ingredients to cook over medium heat until the tips are softened and the shallots are aromatic, then add the brandy.

Allow flames to cook down, then add the chicken stock. Let simmer for 20 minutes and then cool.

Puree in blender or with handheld mixer, strain and return to head. Add the heavy cream and allow the sauce to thicken and reduce.

For the stew:

In a sauté pan over medium heat, add the olive oil, corn, red pepper, garlic, spinach, cumin and salt and pepper, and allow to simmer for approximately 5 minutes.

Add the cream, sugar and salt and pepper to taste.

To plate: Place a small amount of the stew in the center of the plate. Add two medallions of grouper and circle with the asparagus sauce.

177

Seared Salmon
With Braised Napa Cabbage

Ginn Reunion Resort
Orlando, Florida

Christian Schmidt, Executive Chef

Serves 4

Ingredients:

4 - 6 ounce skinless, boneless salmon filets
Fresh fine-grated white pepper corns
¼ cup soy sauce
¼ cup fresh lime juice
2 ounces salmon caviar
3 ounces crème fraiche or sour cream
½ lb Napa cabbage, cleaned and chopped
   coarsely
2 Tbls butter
½ Tbls vegetable oil

To prepare:

Season the filets lightly with pepper on both sides. Pre-heat pan to medium heat and add the vegetable oil.

Add the filets belly side down first and sear on both sides until they are golden brown.

Remove carefully excess oil, keeping the filets in the pan. Add the soy sauce and lime juice. Deglaze while turning the fillets, and cook for another 3-5 minutes per side for medium.

Pre-heat a second pan, melt the butter and add the cabbage. Sauté quickly and season with pepper. Set aside.

To finish:

Place cabbage on dinner plate. Lean a fillet to the side. Top with crème fraiche or sour cream and the salmon caviar.

Sauteed Skate Wing
With Scotch Lentils, Caper and Black Butter Sauce

Orchid Island Golf & Beach Club
Vero Beach, Florida

Jeff McKinney, Executive Chef

Serves 2

Ingredients:

For the skate:
8 oz skate wing
½ cup all purpose flour
Salt and pepper
3 Tbls canola oil

For the Scotch lentils:
1 Tbls butter
1 cup minced onions
2 cloves garlic, minced
1 cup French green lentil
1 bay leaf
3 cup chicken stock
¼ cup Scotch

For the Caper and Black Butter Sauce:
1/4 pound (1 stick) unsalted butter
1 each lemon zest and juice
1 Tbls caper
1 Tbls chopped parsley
Salt and pepper to taste

To Prepare:

For the skate:
Cut the skate wing in 2 – 4 oz portions, season and dredge in flour

Heat oil in sauté pan, sauté the skate wing

about 3-4 minutes till golden brown.

For the Scotch lentils:
Melt the butter in medium saucepan and saute onions until golden brown.

Add garlic, sauté for a few minutes.

Add lentils, bay leaf and chicken stock. Bring it to boil and simmer for about 20 to 30 minutes until tender.

Discard bay leaf, seasoning with salt and pepper and set aside

Shortly before serving, reheat the lentil and stir in the scotch and serve

For the Caper and Black Butter Sauce:
Melt the butter in a sauté pan and cook gently until brown to dark color. Add the rest of the ingredients and heat until warm.

To serve: Create a bed of the lentils and place a skate wing on top. Pour the caper sauce on top

Sweet Potato Crusted Cod
With Vanilla Cream Sauce

Croasdaile Country Club
Durham, North Carolina

Tim Gauldin, Executive Chef

Serves 4

Ingredients:

4 7-8 ounce fillets of cod, skin and bones removed

Sweet Potato Batter:

3 sweet potatoes,
   roasted and peeled
1 Tbls fresh lemon
   juice
1 ½ Tbls fresh orange
   juice
1 Tbls unsalted
   butter
1 tsp salt
½ tsp fresh ginger,
   minced

Pecan-Graham Cracker Crust:

1 cup graham
   crackers, ground
2 cups pecans,
   roasted and ground
4 Tbls unsalted butter, melted

Vanilla Cream Sauce:

½ cup heavy cream
½ vanilla bean, insides removed
Pinch of black pepper
Pinch of salt

To prepare:

Roast sweet potatoes in oven approximately 30-40 minutes or until soft. Allow to cool

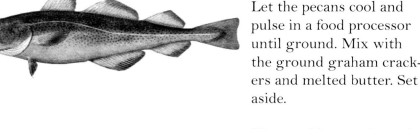

slightly and remove skin. In a food processor puree the potatoes with the juices, butter, salt and ginger. Set aside.

For the crust, begin by roasting the pecans in the oven at 250° for approximately 15 minutes, being careful not to burn. Let the pecans cool and pulse in a food processor until ground. Mix with the ground graham crackers and melted butter. Set aside.

Thoroughly coat the cod fillets with the sweet potato batter, then cover the top and sides with the pecan mixture. Place on a greased baking sheet and bake at 350° for 20 - 25 minutes.

While the fish is cooking place the heavy cream and the vanilla bean pulp in a sauté pan. Bring to a boil and reduce by half. Add salt and pepper and set aside.

Place each finished cod on a plate and top with the vanilla cream sauce.

Serve with sautéed sugar-snap peas or fresh green beans for a splash of color.

Sweet Potato Crusted Trout

The Verandah Grill at The Partridge Inn
Augusta, Georgia

Bradley Czajka, Executive Chef

Serves 4

Ingredients:

8 trout fillets
3 whipped egg whites
Sweet Potato Crust, see below
2 Tbls olive oil

Sweet Potato Crust:
1 sweet potato, sliced thinly
½ butternut squash, sliced thinly
1 cup Panko (Japanese bread crumbs)

To prepare:

Fry sweet potatoes in 300° fryer until they reach a light golden color (be careful not to burn). Can saute instead if desired.

Fry butternut squash the same way.

Allow chips to dry completely overnight.

Grind them up in a food processor with ½ cup of Panko each time that you grind.

Pace in a sealed container and reserve.

Season trout fillets with salt and pepper.

Dip each fillet in whipped egg white mix. Coat evenly in the sweet potato crust.
Pan sear the fish in olive oil to golden brown and finish in a 350° oven until the fish flakes when touched with a fork.

Serve with wilted spinach and homemade mashed potatoes.

Thai Tuna
With Wasabi Mash, Bok-Choy and Thai Stick
Prestonwood Country Club
Cary, North Carolina

Xavier Gomez, Executive Chef

Serves 4

To prepare:

For the tuna:
4 Yellow-fin Tuna filets
Pan sear to desired temperature with oil, salt & pepper on flat top griddle or grill. Set aside and keep warm.

For the Wasabi Mash:
Make a batch of **mashed potatoes** for four. Stir in **sour cream** and some **wasabi** to taste (the potatoes should have a nice kick!).

For the Bok-Choy
Wash some whole **baby bok-choy**, season with minced **garlic, butter and salt and pepper** and steam.

For the Thai stick:
5-inch spring roll wrappers
1 head white cabbage (julienne)
2 large carrots (julienne)
1 case shitake mushrooms (sliced)
Cook the vegetables over high heat in a wok for approx. 1 minute. Be careful not to over-crowd the pan--you may have to do 2 or 3 batches.

Thai sauce for stick:
Garlic, minced
Scallions, thinly sliced
1 tbls ginger, minced
2 tbls sambal (chili paste)
3 tbls sugar
3 tbls soy sauce
1/2 cup mirin
2 Tbls fish sauce
2 limes juiced
2 Tbls corn starch

Whisk all ingredients in large bowl and then lightly boil in wok for 2 minutes. Toss in pre- cooked vegetables and mix thoroughly with boiling sauce, Coat evenly then cool.

Roll cooled vegetable mixture into spring roll with whole leaves of cilantro on the seam approx 4 inches long and 1/2 inch thick (approx 2 oz of vegetable mixture with each spring roll). Seal seam with egg wash.

To serve: Create a bed with potatoes and bok choy, add a few slices of tuna, the Thai stick and drizzle with sauce.

182

Verandah Ahi Tuna
In Citrus Ponzu Sauce and Soy Lime Vinaigrette

The Bonita Bay Club
Bonita Springs, Florida
Tony Larsen, Executive Chef
Serves 4

Ingredients:

For the tuna (per portion):
2 ounces large loin tuna
2 ounces avocado
1 Tbls radish, chopped
1 ounce Ponzu Sauce (below)
1 Tbls chili oil
½ ounce Soy Lime
  Vinaigrette (below)
1 slice plantain
1 pinch micro greens

For the ponzu sauce:
¾ cup sweet mirin
½ cup rice vinegar
4 Tbls soy sauce
½ cup bonito flakes
1 Tbls yuzu zest
¼ cup yuzu juice

For the soy lime vinaigrette:
2 Tbls lime juice
1 tsp soy sauce
2 Tbls sesame oil
2 Tbls peanut oil
(Most ingredients can be found in Asian section of your local market).

To prepare:

For the tuna:
Clean any blood from tuna, cut into 2" strips and toss in soy vinaigrette (see below).

Brunoise avacado and set aside.

Slice radishes thin and reserve in cold water. Slice plantain thin and fry crispy. Season with salt and pepper then reserve.

For the ponzu sauce:
Mix all ingredients together and refrigerate

For the soy lime vinaigrette:
Mix all ingredients together and refrigerate.

To serve: Add Citrus Ponzu to bottom of bowl then layer avacado and tuna together. Use radish, fried plantain and micro greens as garnish.

183

Wonton Crusted Salmon
With Ginger Soy Beurre Blanc

Harmony Golf Preserve
Harmony, Florida
Kelvin Fitzpatrick, Executive Chef
Serves 6

Ingredients:

6 fresh center-cut salmon fillets, 6-8 oz.
each

For the Salmon:
2 cups vegetable oil for frying
20 2" x 2" wonton wrappers
Sesame seeds
4 large eggs
2 Tbls toasted sesame oil
1 cup flour
5 Tbls salt
5 Tbls pepper

For the Ginger Soy Sauce:
½ pound (2 sticks) unsalted butter
2 Tbls fresh ginger
3 cloves, fresh garlic
8 scallions
2 Tbls vegetable oil
1 cup rice wine
1 bay leaf
Salt, white pepper, cayenne pepper to taste
½ cup heavy cream
2 Tbls soy sauce
2 Tbls sugar

To prepare:

For the Sauce:
Cut butter into one-inch cubes and set aside to soften

Mince ginger and garlic. Thinly slice scallions on the bias, separating green from white parts.

Saute ginger and garlic in vegetable oil in a sauce pan until golden brown. Add the rice wine, white part of the scallions, bay leaf, salt, pepper and cayenne pepper. Reduce the wine au sec (almost dry).

Add heavy cream, soy sauce and sugar and reduce over medium heat by one-half.

Reduce heat to low and slowly whisk in one-half of the butter cubes, being careful not to break the sauce. Remove from heat and incorporate the remaining half of the butter.

Adjust seasoning, strain sauce into a container and store at room temperature.

For the Salmon:
Heat oil in sauce pan over medium heat.

Fry wontons until golden brown. Remove from oil onto paper towels and cool completely. Reserve oil in a bowl and set aside.

Place sesame seeds in saute pan and dry toast over medium heat until golden brown. Remove from pan and cool completely.

Grind wontons and sesame seeds in food processor or blender until mixture resembles a fine bread crumb.

Combine sesame oil and eggs in a bowl and whisk until frothy and well incorporated.

Set up a breading procedure with flour in the first bowl, egg mixture in the second, and wonton mixture in the third. Be sure to season each bowl with salt and pepper.

Heat saute pan over medium heat with 1/2 cup of the reserved oil. Season each salmon fillet with salt and pepper.

Dust one salmon filet in flour and shake dry. Then dip the dusted salmon fillet into the egg mixture and shake off excess egg. Immediate-ly dip the salmon into the wonton crumbs and coat evenly. Set salmon on a plate or platter. Repeat process with remaing salmon filets.

Place two breaded fillets into preheated oil in the sauté pan and cook three minutes on each side for medium rare. Be sure and drop the fillets into the pan away from you to avoid oil spatter burns.

After salmon is cooked, remove from pan and drain on paper towels to absorb excess oil. Repeat process with remaining salmon fillets.

To serve: pour one ounce of Ginger Soy Beurre Blanc in a circle around the center of the plate. Scoop four ounces of steamed jasmine rice in the center of the plate and surround with steamed baby bock choy sautéed with bacon. Place a salmon fillet on top.
Finish by drizzling one ounce of sauce on the salmon and garnish with julienne green on-ions remaining from the beurre blanc recipe.

Yellowtail Snapper on Vine-Ripened Tomato Vinaigrette With Grilled Vidalia Onion Guacamole

PGA National Resort & Spa
Palm Beach Gardens, Florida

John Sexton, Executive Chef
Serves 4

Ingredients:

4 8-ounce portions of Yellowtail Snapper

For the Tomato Vinaigrette:
2 large, ripe tomatoes, diced
¼ cup Vidalia onion, minced
½ tsp garlic, minced
3 Tbls Balsamic vinegar
1/3 cup fresh basil, minced
2 Tbls fresh herbs of choice, (thyme, cilantro, etc.)
Fresh ground pepper to taste
2 Tbls extra-virgin olive oil

For the Guacamole:
1 large Vidalia onion, sliced thick
2 Tbls extra-virgin olive oil
2 avocados, diced
1 clove garlic, minced
2 Tbls cilantro, minced
Juice of 2 key limes
2 key limes
Sea salt & pepper to taste

For the Guacamole:
Slice the Vidalia onion, marinate in olive oil and salt, and grill.

Chop the onion and mix well with the rest of the guacamole ingredients.

Season to taste.

For the fish:
Grill the fresh snapper on a hot grill, don't overcook.

Serve on a bed of the tomato vinaigrette and spoon the guacamole on top.

Garnish with key lime wedge.

To prepare:

For the Tomato Vinaigrette:
Mix all ingredients together, season to taste, set aside.

Yellowtail Snapper en Papillote
With Tarragon Compound Butter

Boca Pointe Country Club
Boca Raton, Florida
Terry Daniels, Executive Chef
Serves 4

Ingredients:

For the Tarragon Compound Butter
1 tsp Worcestershire sauce
1 lemon (zest half and fine chop, juice whole lemon)
½ pound (2 sticks) unsalted butter
8 sprigs fresh tarragon, chopped fine
Sea salt and fresh ground black pepper to taste

For the snapper:
4 fresh yellowtail snapper fillets (about 8 ounces, skinned and pin bone removed)
1 bulb fennel (julienne)
6 artichoke hearts, quartered
12 large asparagus (blanched)
8 cherry tomatoes (cut in half)
1 shallot (sliced thin)
8 Kalamata olives
1 lemon (sliced, seeded)
4 parchment paper rounds cut to 16 inch diameter (or wax paper)
Pan spray
Sea salt and fresh ground black pepper

To prepare:

For the Tarragon Compound Butter
Mix all ingredients together. Spread onto a piece of parchment paper and roll into a stick. Refrigerate.

For the snapper:
Prepare all the ingredients for the dish and sauté the fennel until tender. Mix the fennel, artichoke, asparagus, tomatoes, shallot and olives in a mixing bowl with extra virgin olive oil, black pepper and a little sea salt.

Season the fish fillets with salt and pepper. Then place fillets length-wise and off center on a baking pan with parchment paper.

Lay two slices of lemon directly on the fish and then evenly distribute the seasoned vegetable mixture on the fish.

Cut two generous tablespoon-size chunks of tarragon compound butter, remove paper, and place on top of the seasoned vegetable mix.

Fold the paper over the fish and begin to fold and crimp the end of the paper, to seal it. Continue moving around the paper until you reach the other end.

Place on a sprayed sheet tray and bake in a preheated oven of 375° for 25 minutes or until done.

This dish should go from the oven to the table. Once in front of the guest cut the top of the bag and enjoy.

Shellfish
Butter-Poached Lobster Tail
With Fennel-Onion Confit, Parsley Coulis and Potato Disk

Addison Reserve Country Club
Delray Beach, Florida

Sean Key, Executive Chef

Serves 4

Ingredients:

For the Lobster:
4 10-ounce Caribbean lobster tails out of the shell and split length wise
3 cups beurre monte (see below)

For the Fennel Onion Confit:
1 ½ pounds fennel, core removed and julienned in quarter-inch strips
8 ounces yellow onion peeled and julienned in quarter-inch strips
6 Tbls butter, cubed
2 Tbls Italian parsley, chopped
¼ cup water

For the Parsley Coulis:
4 bunches Italian parsley
Water for blanching
Salt and pepper to taste

For the Beurre Monte:
½ cup water
2 pounds (8 sticks) butter

For the Potato Disk:
1 Yukon Gold potato
4 Tbls clarified butter

To prepare:

For the Fennel Onion Confit:
In a medium sauce pan heat water over medium heat and whisk in butter till melted.

Add fennel and onions, cover with parchment and simmer on low for two hours.

After two hours add parsley, season with salt and pepper and set aside, keeping warm.

For the Parsley Coulis:
Discard parlsey stems, blanch leaves briefly in boiling salted water and refresh in ice water.

Squeeze out excess water and blend in a blender with just enough water to puree smooth.

Strain through a medium strainer to remove any large solids and season with salt and pepper.Reserve until assembly.

For the Beurre Monte:
In a very hot sauce pan, add water, remove

188

from heat and whisk in butter a little at a time.

Reserve warm until assembly.

For the Potato Disk:
Preheat oven to 300°.

Slice potato paper thin on a mandoline.

On a parchment-lined sheet pan, brush each side of potato with butter and overlap slices by creating a half disk.

Bake for 30 to 40 minutes until crisp and golden brown.

To serve:
Submerge lobster in Beurre Monte in a small sauce pan on lowest heat until cooked through, about seven minutes.

Heat Coulis in a small sauté pan over medium heat until boiling, add one tablespoon of Beurre Monte and whisk in.

Check seasoning and put two spoonfuls of Coulis in the middle of a warm serving plate.

Top with fennel onion cnfit and place lobster on top of the mixture.

Citrus Salsa Crab Cakes

Royal Oak Resort & Golf Club
Titusville, Florida

Pascal Beaute, Executive Chef

Serves 4

Ingredients:

1 grapefruit

2 oranges

1 red pepper

1 green pepper

1 Vidalia onion

1 bunch of scallions

1 large tomato

½ bunch of cilantro

1 Tbls jalapeno
pepper, chopped

1 Tbls garlic,
chopped

½ bunch of fresh
parsley

2 pounds lump crab
meat

½ pound of bread
crumbs

1 cup of mayonnaise

Salt and pepper to
taste

To prepare:

For the salsa:
Peel the orange and grapefruit, cut in sections then in small pieces, removing the white skin (membrane).

Cut half of the red and green pepper, half the onion, the scallion and the tomato in small dices of about ¼ inch. Fine chop the cilantro. Mix all together, adding salt and pepper as needed. Set aside.

For the crab cakes:
Place the rest of the peppers and onions, garlic,and parsley in a food processor and blend it finely. Take that mixture and mix with the crab, the mayonnaise and the bread crumbs. Taste for seasoning.

Heat a sauté pan to medium heat. Using a tablespoon or an ice cream scoop, drop the crab cakes on the pan, flipping them after 2 minutes to brown the other side.

Serve on a plate with the salsa on the side.

Crab and Flounder
With Green Beans & Brown Butter Cream

Daufuskie Island Resort
Daufuskie Island, South Carolina
Andrew Geller, Executive Chef

Serves 6

Ingredients:

12 3-ounce pieces of Flounder fillets
12 ounces blue crab meat
2 tsps Old Bay seasoning
2 Tbls finely diced celery
2 Tbls finely diced onion
2 Tbls finely diced red bell pepper
2 Tbls mayonnaise
1 pound green beans, cleaned and blanched
1 cup toasted almond slivers
1 pound (4 sticks) unsalted butter
2 cups heavy cream
Olive oil
All-purpose flour
Kosher salt and freshly ground black
  pepper

To prepare:

Squeeze all excess water out of crab meat and remove any remaining pieces of shell.

In a small bowl mix crab meat with celery, onion, pepper, Old Bay and mayonnaise. Set aside.

Season flounder fillets with salt and pepper and lightly dredge in flour. In a large skillet over medium heat sauté filets in olive oil for 3 minutes on each side achieving a nice golden brown color, then remove from pan and place on a paper towel to degrease. Keep the pan handy.

Continue process until all fillets are done.

Place in 250° oven to keep warm while finishing sauce.

In a small saucepan add 8 ounces of butter and cook over low heat until the butter turns brown. Add 2 cups of cream and continue to cook over low heat whisking to incorporate butter and cream together. Season with salt and pepper to taste.

In the large skillet in which the fish were sauteed, pour out any grease and wipe clean of any remaining flour. Add 2 ounces of butter and the green beans and cook over medium heat, tossing occasionally to heat beans through. Season with salt and pepper to taste.

To plate, place 4 ounces of brown butter cream in center of plate. Add a layer of green beans on the plate, place one fillet on the beans, spoon the crab mixture onto the fillet and then top with a second fillet piece. Sprinkle with toasted almonds and serve.

191

Divers Scallops
With Butternut Squash, Heirloom Tomato Concasse and Fresh Mint

San Jose Country Club
Jacksonville, Florida

Jean-Christophe Setin, Executive Chef

Serves 2

Ingredients:

4 U10 scallops (dry pack or fresh)
1 butternut squash
2 large heirloom tomatoes, peeled
Extra virgin olive oil,
Salt and cracked pepper
2 oz heavy cream
2 sprigs of fresh mint
1 sprig of thyme
2 Tbls butter

To prepare:

Peel and dice the butternut squash, place in an oven proof dish and drizzle with olive oil, salt and pepper. Roast in 350° oven until tender. When done, place on a cutting board and chop roughly into medium-size chunks. Set aside and keep warm.

Cut the peeled tomatoes in half and squeeze the seeds out. Dice and place in an ovenproof pot with some olive oil and the sprig of thyme. Allow to get hot on the stove and then place in a 325° oven. Bake until all natural water has disappeared.

Season the scallops. In a skillet, heat olive oil until smoky, add butter and immediately sear the scallops for 1 minute on both sides. Remove from the skillet and place on a paper towel.

Chop the fresh mint and mix with micro greens.

To serve: Plate the scallops with the squash, add a spoonful of the tomato concasse and garnish with the mint and greens.

WINE SUGGESTION: Newton Unfiltered, Napa Valley, California

192

First Coast Crab Cakes
With Key Lime Beurre Blanc and Cajun Remoulade
Doublegate Country Club
Albany, Georgia

Robert K. Bell, Executive Chef
Serves 8-10

Ingredients:

For the Crab Cakes:
1 box Carr's Crackers,* crushed
1 pound lump crab meat
1 pound jumbo lump crab
4-5 egg whites
Juice of 2 lemons
1 Tbls parsley, chopped
1 cup mayonnaise
Sea salt and white pepper, to taste

For the Cajun Remoulade:
1 cup mayonnaise
¼ cup dill relish
1 Tbls capers, chopped
Juice of 1 lemon
1 tsp Tabasco sauce
Worcestershire sauce, to taste
1 Tbls Cajun spice

For the Key Lime Beurre Blanc:
1 cup dry white wine
1 shallot, chopped
12 black peppercorns
4 ounces heavy cream
1 Tbls lime juice
2 sticks (1/2 lb) sweet butter, cubed and
    chilled

For the Fresh Salsa:
2 tomatoes, diced
1 red onion, chopped
1 tsp garlic, chopped
1 fresh hot pepper
2 tsp cilantro, chopped
1 Tbls red wine vinegar
1 Tbls olive oil
* Carr's® Assorted Biscuits for Cheese 7.5oz

Box

To prepare:

For the Salsa: Mix together all ingredients and chill well.

For the Remoulade: Mix together and chill. Will keep for several weeks.

For the Crab Cakes: Mix all ingredients and form into 1-2 ounce cakes. Sauté in a light vegetable oil, lightly brown on both sides. Finish in a hot oven 375-400° for 5 to 7 minutes.

For the Beurre Blanc: Reduce wine, shallots and peppercorns on low heat until 3/4 reduced. Add heavy cream. Reduce by half. Add lime juice, whip in chilled butter. Strain. Finish with Cajun spice. Hold sauce in warm spot. Sauce will break if it gets too hot.

To plate: Place crab cakes on beurre blanc, top with the remoulade and garnish with the salsa.

193

Glazed Lump Crab

Gasparilla Inn & Club
Boca Grande, Florida
James Dyer, Executive Chef
Serves 4

Ingredients:

1/4 pound (1 stick) butter
2 Tbls chicken stock
1 Tbls white wine
2 Tbls shallots, minced
1 pound lump crab
Salt and pepper to taste
Wilted spinach, as needed
4 slices Virginia ham, thinly sliced
4 Holland rusk (toasted bread rounds)

Hollandaise sauce (see recipe p. 131)

To prepare:

Combine butter, chicken stock, white wine and shallots in a sauté pan. Cook and shake over high heat until thick and creamy. Be sure to have the pan in constant motion until the emulsion is thick and creamy.

Remove the pan from the heat and stir in the crab. Place back over low heat and warm through. Remove to a warm place.

To serve: Squeeze out the wilted spinach and place on a ham slice. Place the slice on the Holland rusk. Top with crab. Top this with the hollandaise and glaze underneath the broiler.

Serve immediately.

Lobster Savannah

Dataw Island Club
Dataw Island, South Carolina

Joe Kelly, Executive Chef
Serves 2

Ingredients:

1 ½ lobster, boiled 6 minutes in white
    wine, water and shallots (reserve water
    as stock)
½ cup heavy cream
¼ cup beurre manie
Pinch of dill
2 ounces red pepper, diced
2 ounces green pepper, diced
2 ounces yellow pepper, diced
2 ounces mushrooms
4 ounces scallops
4 ounces swordfish
4 ounces tuna
4 ounces grouper
4 ounces shrimp
4 ounces crabmeat cooked in lobster stock
Bearnaise sauce
Parmesan cheese

To prepare:

Add ½ cup heavy cream to 2 cups of the hot
lobster stock. Whisk in ¼ cup beurre manie
(equal portions of margarine and flour mixed
well) until smooth. Add a pinch of dill, the
peppers and mushrooms and simmer for 2
minutes. Add in seafood and bring to a boil.

Cut lobster in half lengthwise, remove the tail
meat, reserve, and wash out the shell cavity.
Place seafood mixture in the center cavity and
top with bearnaise sauce and parmesan cheese.
Bake at 450° until brown. Place the lobster tail
meat on top of shell and garnish with mussels
and crawfish.

*Suggested wines: Louis Jadot Beaujolais Village
or Sonoma Cutter Chardonnay*

Pancetta Wrapped Shrimp
With Creamy Mascarpone Polenta

Jacksonville Golf & Country Club
Jacksonville, Florida

Ingredients:

20 large shrimp (16-20 Count), peeled &
    deveined, tails left on
1 large shallot, minced
2 cloves garlic, minced
4 large basil leaves, coarsely chopped
1 lb (or 20 slices) Pancetta ham, sliced thin
1 pinch, crushed red pepper
1 8 oz tub, Mascarpone cheese
1/4 pound (1 stick) unsalted butter, cut
    into pats
1 cup Marsala wine
1 cup polenta corn meal
2 cups whole milk
2 cups water
2 Tbls extra-virgin olive oil
Salt & Pepper to taste

Michael Ramsey, Executive Chef
Serves 4

To prepare:

For the Shrimp:
On a cutting board, slice the pancetta down
the middle, 3/4 through and flip down to
make one long narrow piece. Season shrimp
with pepper and wrap in the pancetta, leaving
head and tail exposed, Set aside.

For the Polenta:
Bring milk and water seasoned with salt and
pepper to a light boil in a heavy saucepan.
Reduce heat to medium and slowly add the
polenta while whisking. Switch to a wooden
spoon and stir constantly. When the mixture
bubbles, reduce heat to low and continue to
stir every couple of minutes so that it doesn't
stick to the bottom of the pan.

To finish the polenta, stir in the mascarpone
and half of the butter, seasoning if needed.
To Finish:
In a large cast-iron skillet, heat olive oil. Carefully place wrapped shrimp in a layer without
overcrowding, cooking in batches if needed.
After one minute, flip the shrimp and cook for
another minute. Remove the shrimp from the
pan and put on a plate to rest.

Add the shallot, garlic, and crushed red pepper
to the skillet and sauté over medium heat until
shallots are translucent.

Add the Marsala and return the shrimp to the
pan. Reduce the Marsala until only a half cup
remains. Add the chopped basil and stir in the
rest of the butter. Turn off heat and taste
sauce, seasoning if necessary.

To serve: Pour the polenta into a large platter
or casserole dish and top with shrimp. Spoon
the sauce over the shrimp and serve.

Seared Scallops
With Tabasco Gastrique and Stir-Fry Vegetables

Musgrove Country Club
Jasper, Alabama
Phil Schirle, Executive Chef
Yield: 12 portions

Ingredients:
60 U-10 sea scallops
5 ounces Tabasco Sauce
1 pound granulated sugar
1 Tbls Creole seasoning

For the Stir-Fried Vegetables:
1 cup baby corn
1 cup Shiitake mushrooms (caps sliced)
1 cup sugar-snap peas
1 cup baby carrots (peeled and steamed)
1 cup red bell pepper (thin julienne)

For the Stir-Fry Sauce:
1 cup Teriyaki sauce
½ cup soy sauce
2 Tbls sesame oil
1 Tbls garlic, minced
1 Tbls fresh ginger, minced
2 ounces Tabasco sauce
3 tsps corn starch

12 Puff Pastry Vol-au-Vent (round, fillable puff pastries)

To prepare:
Peel side muscle off of the scallops, toss with Creole seasoning and set aside.

For the Gastrique: Combine Tabasco sauce and the granulated sugar in a heavy bottom saucepan. Place on low flame and cook until sugar is melted. Increase flame to medium-high and cook until sauce starts bubbling. Reserve.

For the Stir-Fry Sauce: Combine all ingredients in saucepan, bring to boil, thicken with cornstarch slurry.

In sauté pan, heat 2 ounces olive oil to near smoking. Place seasoned scallops in oil and sear until brown and crusty, approximately 2-3 minutes. Turn scallops over and cook an additional minute. Meanwhile, sauté vegetables until cooked but still crispy, add the stir-fry sauce and cook until sauce glazes the vegetables.

To Serve: Place puff pastry Vol-au-vent in center of plate, spoon the stir-fried vegetables into the puff pastry, Place five scallops around the pastry shell and drizzle the Tabasco Gastrique over and around the scallops. Garnish with thyme sprig and green onion flower.

197

Shrimp and Grits

The Lodge at Sea Island
St. Simons Island, Georgia

Johannes Klapdohr, Executive Chef

Serves 4

Ingredients:

For the Shrimp:

1 pound fresh local shrimp (Size: 21-25), shelled and deveined.

2 Tbls shallots, finely cut

3 vine-ripe tomatoes, skinned, quartered, seeded and diced

1 Tbls olive oil

½ Tbls parsley, finely cut

½ Tbls basil, finely cut

½ Tbls chives, finely cut

½ cup white wine

1 cup chicken stock

4 Tbls butter

Salt and pepper to taste

For the grits:

2 quarts water

1 quart half & half

½ pound (2 sticks) butter

3 cups white corn grits

1 pound fresh corn, preferable sweet or Florida silver corn

Salt and pepper to taste

To prepare:

Cook the grits first.

Boil the water, heavy cream and butter, and season with salt and pepper. Stir in grits and return to boil. Simmer over low heat for 10 minutes until thickened. Grits should be nice and creamy.

Sauté fresh-shucked corn in a pan with some butter until lightly golden and combine with the grits. Make sure grits is fully cooked; set aside and keep warm.

(Note: The recipe calls for what seems like a lot of water, but the grits will absorb it!)

For the shrimp:

Bring a 14" pan up to high heat on stove. Add a splash of olive oil and coat the pan. Carefully add shrimp and sauté. They will curl up and change color to pink. Be careful not to over cook! Season with salt and pepper, set aside in a colander and reserve the liquid.

In the same pan, sweat the shallots with butter. Add the tomatoes and fresh herbs. Deglaze with white wine. Add the shrimp liquid and chicken stock and reduce.
Reduce the heat and bind the sauce with the butter. Add the shrimp back into the sauce and coat them. Do not overcook.

To plate: Spoon the creamy, buttery corn grits onto the plate and top with the shrimp with the sauce. Garnish with fresh herbs.

Shrimp Carbonara

Arnold Palmer's Bay Hill Club & Lodge
Orlando, Florida

Robert Lee, Executive Chef
Serves 2

Ingredients:

10 jumbo shrimp
½ tsp chopped garlic
½ tsp chopped shallots
1/3 cup diced prosciutto
¼ cup spring peas
1 cup heavy cream
½ cup grated Parmesan
   cheese
1 egg yolk
Angel hair pasta for 2
Salt and pepper to taste

To prepare:

Sauté shrimp in a small amount of olive oil for two minutes, turning once.

Add prosciutto, garlic and shallots and sauté for 30 seconds. Add peas and heavy cream and bring to a boil. Whisk in one egg yolk. Add Parmesan cheese, salt and pepper.

Heat pasta, and divide the shrimp and sauce into two servings.

199

Voodoo Shrimp With Cream Sauce

Green Meadow Country Club
Alcoa, Tennessee

Charles David Mills, Executive Chef
Serves 4

Ingredients:

1 can Guinness beer (or dark beer of your choice)
¼ cup shallots
¼ cup garlic, minced
2 rosemary sprigs
¼ tsp dried rosemary
3 bay leaves
1 lemon, juiced
½ bottle Worcestershire sauce
1 quart heavy cream
1 Tbls shrimp base
2 pounds 16-20 count shrimp, peeled and deveined, tails on
Blonde roux as needed
Water as needed
Unsalted butter as needed

To prepare:

Reduce beer, shallots and garlic to a syrup. Add the rest of the ingredients except for the roux, butter and shrimp. Bring to a boil, then reduce to a simmer for 20 minutes.

While sauce is simmering, bring water to a boil in a medium sauce pan and add the shrimp. Cook until done, then ice the shrimp down and set aside.

After 20 minutes of simmering the sauce, add some of the blonde roux and thicken the sauce until it can coat the back of a spoon. Remove the bay leaves and rosemary springs and set sauce aside.

In a shallow saucepan or sauté pan, add the butter and shrimp. Saute until the butter is melted and the shrimp are evenly coated. Begin to add some of the voodoo sauce until the shrimp are covered in sauce. Reduce heat and allow to simmer for 5-7 minutes.

Remove from heat and serve. Serve over pasta topped with parmesan cheese, diced tomatoes and scallions or over wild or long-grain rice topped with diced tri-color peppers and red onion.

Warm Blue Crab Enchilada
With Roasted Corn and Papaya Seed Vinaigrette

Card Sound Country Club
Key Largo, Florida

Kevin Cornaire Executive Chef

Serves 4

Ingredients:

For the Enchiladas:

4 8" flour tortillas

1 pound jumbo lump blue crab meat

2 cups shredded cabbage

½ cup shredded carrots

1 bunch diced scallion

1 cup small diced seeded tomato

½ cup shredded Monterey jack cheese

¼ cup dry white wine

Salt and pepper to
    taste

¼ cup corn oil or
    canola

*For the Roasted Corn
Papaya Seed Vinaigrette:*

2 cups sweet corn
    (roasted)

3 ounces rice wine
    vinegar

1 cup corn oil or
    canola oil

2 ounces honey

¼ cup finely chopped cilantro

½ cup papaya seeds

¼ tsp turmeric

¼ tsp cumin

Salt and pepper to taste

To prepare:

For the Roasted Corn Papaya Seed Vinaigrette:
Combine roasted corn, salt and pepper, vinegar, honey, cilantro, papaya seeds, turmeric, and cumin in blender. Run blender on high and slowly drizzle in oil until an emulsion is formed.

For the Enchiladas:
In a large skillet sauté crab, cabbage, carrots, half of the scallions, and ½ cup tomato for about 2 minutes. Season to taste.

Add wine and cook 30 seconds. Add cheese to bind.

Warm flour tortillas in microwave (about 15-20 seconds) or in low oven until supple. Spoon crab mixture into tortillas, fold ends and roll.

Cut in half and garnish with corn vinaigrette and remaining tomato and scallions.

Desserts

Everyone says "Oh, no dessert for me...I'm too full!" Of course, everyone lies!

That's why we asked the chefs for their most tempting recipes for cakes, pies, puddings and cookies. Go ahead and splurge...you deserve it!

Apple Cake

Atlantic Room, Kiawah Island Resort
Kiawah Island, South Carolina

Randy MacDonald, Executive Chef

Ingredients:

2 ½ cups flour
2 cups sugar
½ tsp cinnamon
2 tsp baking powder
1 tsp salt
4 each eggs
1 ¼ cups oil
1 tsp vanilla
3 cups diced apples
1 cup chopped pecans

To prepare:

Mix all dry ingredients in mixing bowl. Add eggs one at a time, oil next, and then vanilla. Fold in apples and pecans.

Spray the inside of the bundt pan with cooking spray and pour cake batter into it.

Bake at 350° for 1 hour and 10 minutes.

Can be served plain or with a sugar icing.

203

Apples & Almonds
Caramelized in Whiskey and Brown Sugar with Butter Pecan Ice Cream

San Jose Country Club
Jacksonville, Florida
Jean-Christophe Setin, Executive Chef
Serves 2

Ingredients:

2 Granny Smith apples
1 cup dark brown sugar
6 Tbls unsalted butter
1 cup Jack Daniels bourbon
½ cup of sliced, blanched almonds
Butter pecan ice cream
Cinnamon sugar

To prepare:

Peel and core the apples and cut then in 8 sections.

In a skillet, heat the butter and let it get to the brown stage. Add the apples and saute until they start to get caramelized on the side. Add the brown sugar and keep cooking the apples until the sugar has formed a caramel coat.

Deglaze and flambe with the bourbon. Reduce the liquids until almost dry.

Place the apples in a 3" cast iron marmite or cocotte pot and sprinkle blanched almonds on top. Put the lid down and bake at 350° for 10 minutes.

Take out of the oven remove the lid and lean it against the side. Place a small scoop of ice cream on top and dust with Cinnamom Sugar.

Enjoy with a Chateau du Grand Carretey, Sauternes, 2005.

204

Banana Cream Pie

The Club at St. James Plantation
Southport, North Carolina

John Turner, Executive Chef
Serves 4-6

Ingredients:

For the Crust:
2 ½ cups crushed vanilla wafer cookies
¼ cup mashed banana
¼ cup sugar
½ teaspoon cinnamon
4 Tbls unsalted butter melted

For the Filling :
½ cup sugar
½ cup cornstarch
¼ tsp salt
1 ½ cups whipping cream
1 ½ cups whole milk
3 large egg yolks
½ vanilla bean split lengthwise
2 ½ Tbls unsalted butter
1 tsp vanilla extract
6 ripe bananas about 1 ½ lbs., cut on the
  crosswise about ¼ -inch-thick

To prepare:

For the crust :
Preheat oven to 350°. Stir vanilla wafers, sugar, and mashed banana, in a large bowl and blend. Add unsalted butter and stir mixture. until even. Press onto the bottom and sides of a 10 inch glass pie dish and bake until it reaches a lite golden color and chill until firm, about 25-30 minutes.

For the filling:
Whisk sugar, cornstarch, in a heavy medium saucepan to blend. Slowly whisk in whipping cream and whole milk, then egg yolks. Scrape in seeds from the vanilla bean.

Whisk over moderate heat until custard begins to thicken, and begins to boil (about 6 minutes) Remove from heat. Whisk in unsalted butter and vanilla extract.

Transfer filling to a large bowl; cool completely, whisking a few times within the hour. Stir custard if necessary. Spread a layer the custard and then the bananas, and repeat layering with remaining custard, and bananas.

Chill pie until filling is set, at least 6-7 hours. Serve as is, top with whipped cream, or add a little melted chocolate to the filling.

Bananas Foster Bread Pudding

Musgrove Country Club
Jasper, Alabama

Phil Schirle, Executive Chef
Yield: About 18 servings

Ingredients:

2 loaves French bread, cut ½ inch thick
2 pounds sugar
12 large eggs
1 ounce vanilla extract
3/4 gallon milk
1 pound (4 sticks) unsalted butter – melted
2 cups banana liqueur
12 bananas, sliced

For the Sauce:
1 pound light brown sugar
2/3 pound (2 2/3 sticks) unsalted butter
1 cup heavy cream

To prepare:

Beat sugar, eggs, and vanilla for a long time, until the sugar is dissolved and not grainy. Add the milk and banana liqueur and mix thoroughly. Pour over the cut bread and soak well, leaving no unsoaked bread. Add the sliced bananas and mix to combine

Butter a 2-inch hotel pan and pour the mixture into it. Pour the melted butter over the top of the bread mixture.

Pour 1 ½ to 2 cups of hot water into a second 2-inch hotel pan,.Set the bread pudding pan into the water pan (thus making a double boiler), and place in 325° oven, uncovered, for 1 hour and 45 minutes, until brown.

Wrap entire pan with foil and continue to cook for an additional 30 to 45 minutes until set but not too stiff.

Meanwhile, make the sauce in a separate pan by combining the brown sugar and the butter and cooking over medium heat until the sugar is dissolved and not grainy. Add the heavy cream and bring to a boil. Set aside and keep at room temperature.

When the bread pudding comes out of the oven, allow it to rest for a few minutes and it will "sink" in the pan. Pour the caramel sauce on top of the bread pudding or serve it on the side. Serve warm.

Banana Mango Bread

Hammock Bay Golf & Country Club
Naples, Florida
Desmond McGuire, Executive Chef

Ingredients:

2 cups all-purpose flour
1 tsp baking soda
¼ tsp salt
1/4 pound (1 stick) butter
¾ cup sugar
1 tsp molasses
2 eggs beaten
1 1/3 cups over-ripe bananas - mashed
2/3 cup mango puree

9x5 loaf pan lightly- greased and floured

To prepare:

Pre-heat oven to 350°.

Combine first three ingredients in a large mixing bowl. In a separate bowl cream together butter, sugar and molasses. Once mixture is creamed add in eggs, mango puree and mashed banana.

Gently mix mango and banana mixture into the flour mixture. Stir only until all ingredients are combined.

Pour batter into prepared pan and bake for one hour. Bread is finished when pick inserted into the middle off the loaf comes out clean. Let bread sit in pan for 5 - 10 minutes then remove and cool on wire rack.

Carrot Cake

Delray Dunes Golf & Country Club
Boynton Beach, Florida

Mark LaFrance, Executive Chef
Makes one cake

Ingredients:

4 cups flour
4 cups sugar
1 tsp salt
4 tsp baking soda
6 tsp cinnamon
3 cups Crisco oil
6 cups grated carrots
4 tsp of vanilla
8 eggs

To prepare:

Cream sugar, oil and eggs, then add dry ingredients and fold in carrots.

Bake at 375° in a greased pan until done. Check in 30-45 minutes.

Icing:
Combine 2 sticks of butter, 1 ½ boxes of powdered sugar and 16 oz. of cream cheese.

Danish Aebleskivers

Grande Oaks Country Club
Fort Lauderdale, Florida

Jeff Masanz, Executive Chef
4-6 Servings

Ingredients:

For the Aebleskivers:
3 each whole eggs (separated)
2 cups buttermilk
1½ cups all purpose flour
2 tsp baking powder
1 Tbls granulated sugar
½ tsp salt
¼ tsp cinnamon
2 Tbls unsalted butter, melted
1 each sliced banana (24 pieces)

For the Strawberry sauce:
**1 pint fresh strawberries (slice all and
    reserve half)**
1½ cups granulated sugar
1 cup water

For the Candied Lemon Zest:
1 each large lemon
½ cup water
1¼ cups sugar

To prepare:

For the Strawberry sauce:
Make simple syrup by boiling sugar and water together and adding half of the strawberries. Puree after 5 minutes of cooking. Toss in rest of strawberries.

For the Candied Lemon Zest:
Boil sugar and water together until thick bubbles form. Using a zest knife, zest lemons making long thin strands. Once simple syrup is ready add zest and let cook for 1 minute. Pull each strand out of pot and place on a cookie sheet sprayed with pan release. Let cool. Be careful: strands are very hot and will burn if touched.

For the Aebleskivers:
Beat egg whites until stiff peaks form and set aside. Beat egg yolks and buttermilk together. Sift all dry ingredients and add to egg yolk mixture.

Add melted butter to liquid mix and beat until smooth. Fold in egg whites using a rubber spatula. Batter is now complete. Next, using an Aebleskiver cast iron pan, (available in specialty stores), fill pan quarter full with oil or shortening, then fill pan cups with batter. Add a slice of banana in the center. Cook over medium-high heat.

Once edges become golden brown, turn with a skewer, or tooth pick.

Place Aebleskivers on plate. Dress with strawberry sauce, powdered sugar, or sweetened whipped cream if desired and garnish with candied lemon zest.

Chocolate Praline Profiteroles

Grand Harbor
Vero Beach, Florida

Timothy Blouin, Head Pastry Chef
Yield: 40 profiteroles

Ingredients:

For the Pate Choux:
1 cup water
1/4 pound (1 stick) butter
Pinch of Salt
5 ounces bread flour
1 cup whole eggs

For the Pralines:
1/2 pound (2 sticks) butter
1 cup brown sugar
2 cups pecans (finely chopped)

For the Ganache:
1 cup heavy cream
8 ounces dark chocolate (chopped)

For the Pastry Cream:
3 cups milk
8 ounces sugar
1 cup milk
3 ounces cornstarch
4 eggs
2 egg yolks
4 Tbls butter
1 tsp vanilla

To prepare:

For the Pate Choux:
Bring water, butter and salt to a boil, add flour and stir until mixture turns into a thick paste and pulls away from the sides of the pot. Remove from heat and put mixture into a mixer, adding eggs slowly and mixing until incorporated.

Put mixture into a pastry bag with a large open tip and pipe the profiteroles about the size of a half dollar on a half sheet pan with parchment paper, allowing enough space between them to double in size. Bake at 350° for about 15 minutes or until golden brown and dry in the center.

For the Pralines:
Melt butter, add the brown sugar and bring to a boil. Turn off the heat, add the pecans and stir until incorporated. Pour mixture onto a half sheet pan with a silicone baking sheet on it and bake at 350° for about 10 minutes until praline is bubbling in the center. Let cool.

For the Ganache:
Bring heavy cream to a boil, pour over chocolate and stir until chocolate is completely melted and ganache is shiny.

210

For the Pastry Cream:
Combine 3 cups milk and sugar and bring to a boil. Add the second portion of milk to the cornstarch and stir to dissolve. Add the eggs and yolks to the cornstarch mixture, temper some of the hot milk into the cornstarch mixture, then add the warmed cornstarch mixture to the milk, and cook over medium heat stirring constantly until mixture thickens and starts to bubble.

Pull off heat, add the butter, vanilla and 3 ounces of the ganache, and gently stir until incorporated. Pour into a shallow pan, cover and chill.

To Serve:
Start by slicing the profiteroles in half so you have a top and a bottom. Break up the praline and add ¾ of it to the chocolate pastry cream and gently fold it in.

With an ice cream scoop; place one scoop of the chocolate praline pastry cream into each of the bottom profiteroles, dip the tops of the profiteroles into the ganache, and place on the pastry cream, then sprinkle the rest of the praline on top and chill until you serve them.

Chocolate Sabayon

Rosen Shingle Creek Resort
Orlando, Florida
Jorge Oliveira, Executive Chef
Serves 2

Ingredients:

½ cup milk chocolate
1 tsp gelatin
3 Tbls Marsala wine
2 Tbls sugar
3 whole eggs
1 ¼ cup whipped cream

To prepare:
Bloom gelatin. Melt chocolate.

Boil marsala wine and sugar until sugar dissolves. Start whipping eggs and pour slowly down the side of the bowl into the boiling marsala mixture. Add the melted chocolate. Melt gelatin and add to the mixture.

Cool mixture down and add whipped cream.

Double-Chocolate Semi-Fredo

Memphis Country Club
Memphis, Tennessee

Kenneth Thompson, Executive Chef
10 servings

Ingredients:

For the Ganache:
6 oz. chocolate, dark coating

3 oz. heavy cream

For the Cake Base:
2.7 oz. cocoa powder
6 oz. hot water
12 oz. sugar
6 oz. all-purpose flour
1 tsp baking soda
1 tsp baking powder
¾ tsp salt
6 oz. milk
3 oz. vegetable oil
½ tsp vanilla extract
1 ½ eggs

For the Mousse:
3.5 oz. sugar
1.5 oz. water
2.5 oz. Pasteurized Egg Yolks
16 oz. heavy cream
6.5 oz, 58% dark chocolate, melted

To prepare:

For the Ganache:
Bring the heavy cream to a boil, remove from heat, and pour over chocolate. Stir mixture until completely incorporated.

Pour mixture into a holding pan to cool.

Once mixture has cooled completely, scoop ten small balls of ganache onto a sheet pan. Cover and refrigerate until needed.

For the Cake Base:
In a small bowl, combine the hot water and cocoa powder to make a slurry.
Combine the remaining dry ingredients in the bowl of an electric mixer.

In a separate bowl, combine the milk, oil, vanilla, and eggs and mix until fully incorporated.

Add the wet ingredients and cocoa slurry to the dry ingredients and mix until fully incorporated.

Using a wire whisk attachment, whip batter on medium speed for two to three minutes. Pour batter onto a flat half-sheet pan lined with parchment paper and sprayed with cooking oil.

Bake cake at 350° for approximately 15 minutes. Once baked, remove the cake from the oven and allow to cool completely.

Using a circle cutter cut out 10 cake rounds the size of the top of the muffin pan.

For the Mousse:
Combine sugar and water in a small pot and cook to 240° over high heat.

Place the pasteurized egg yolks in a small electric mixing bowl with whisk attachment. Once the sugar solution has reached temperature, with the mixer on medium-high speed, slowly pour the solution into the egg yolks and whip at high speed until the bowl is cool to the touch.

In a separate small electric mixing bowl, whip the heavy cream to soft peaks using a whisk attachment.

Alternately, fold the whipped cream and melted chocolate in two parts into the egg yolk mixture until fully incorporated.

For the Bombes:
Immediately after the mousse is made, pour into a pastry bag with a plain tip.
Pipe the mousse into 10 large flexi-mold muffin pans three-quarters of the way full.

Drop the pre-scooped ganache into the center of the mousse, and use a palate knife to even the mold and fully cover the ganache and make level.

Freeze bombes until completely frozen.

To serve:
Unmold the bombe and place onto the pre-cut cake round and on the serving plate.

Garnish with stripes of melted chocolate, caramel sauce, caramelized hazelnuts, fresh berries, sweet cream, and chocolate cigarette.

Feuilletine Crunch

Rosen Shingle Creek Resort
Orlando, Florida

Jorge Oliveira, Executive Chef

Serves 2

Ingredients:

4 cups praline paste
½ cup milk chocolate
¾ cup feuilletine

Note: If praline paste or feuilletine (a chocolate-covered wafer) are not available, substitute peanut butter for the paste and Rice Krispys for the feuilletine.

To prepare:

Melt nut paste. Melt chocolate.

Combine nut paste and melted chocolate

Fold in paste and chocolate with Feuilletine.

Fresh Fruit and Zabalone

Haig Point Club
Daufuskie Island, South Carolina

Gerard Brunett, Executive Chef

Serves 4

Ingredients:

1 pint raspberries
1 pint blackberries
4 strawberries cut in half
3 egg yolks
3 Tbls sugar in the raw
½ cup Grand Marnier
Mint for garnish

To prepare:

In a stainless bowl over a double boiler slowly heat the egg yolks and sugar until dissolved, whisking slowly during the process. Add the liquor and continue to whisk until it becomes thick enough to stick to a spoon. Do not allow it to boil. Remove from heat and let cool approx. 1 hour before service.

Plating: In chilled bowls place equal portions of the fruit. Top with zabalone, garnish with mint and serve.

214

Guinness Ice Cream

Golf Club at Briar's Creek
John's Island, South Carolina

Ingredients:

12 ounces Guinness stout beer
2 cups heavy cream (light cream and half-
    and half not recommended)
2 cups whole milk
¾ cup granulated sugar
1 vanilla bean split in half lengthwise
6 egg yolks

David Tolerton, Executive Chef
Yield: One quart

To prepare:

In large saucepan, simmer the stout until reduced by ¾ the volume, about 8 minutes.

Combine milk, cream, and sugar in a heavy
gauge saucepan. Drop in vanilla bean and
bring to gentle boil over medium heat, then
remove from heat.

In a medium bowl beat egg yolks, whisk in
1 cup of the hot cream mixture then gradually add the yolk mixture to the hot cream
whisking constantly. Put saucepan back on
medium heat until mixture thickens and will
coat the back of a spoon -- it needs to reach
170 degrees (Caution: any higher will result in
scrambled eggs in your ice cream. An instant
read thermometer is highly recommended.)

Remove from heat, strain through mesh
strainer into clean container. Lay some plastic
wrap against the surface to prevent skin from
forming on top of ice cream batter.

Chill at least 4 hours, overnight is better.
Place your Guinness stout reduction in separate container and refrigerate as well at least 4
hours.

Remove ice cream batter and Guinness from
fridge. Whisk in the Guinness to batter until
well blended. Freeze in your ice cream machine to the manufacturers instructions.

Transfer to airtight container and freeze till
ready to serve.

This ice-cream will keep about two weeks in
freezer, although I never had any last that
long! There are no preservatives so remember
to keep airtight to keep out freezer burn.

215

Frozen Chocolate Mousse
With Bruleed Bananas
and Peanut Butter Ice Cream

Atlantic Room at Kiawah Island Resort
Kiawah Island, South Carolina

Randy MacDonald, Executive Chef
Serves 6-10

Ingredients:

For the mousse:
**20 oz good quality bittersweet
  chocolate, chopped**
6 Tbls butter
10 egg yolks
2/3 cup sugar
10 egg whites
1 Tbls vanilla extract
2 cups heavy cream

For the peanut butter ice cream:
1 1/3 cups heavy cream
1 quart half/half
1 vanilla bean, split
1 cup sugar
16 egg yolks
1 cup creamy peanut butter
½ cup chopped roasted peanuts

To prepare:

Melt chocolate and butter in bowl set over barely simmering water. Cool to room temperature.

Whisk yolks with 1/3 cup of sugar and a splash of water and cook to 145° in a bowl over lightly simmering water. Whisk off heat until cool.

Whisk egg whites with 1/3 of the sugar the same way. Beat in mixer until cool. Fold whites into yolks, then fold in chocolate. Whip heavy cream to medium peaks and fold in with vanilla.

In a 3x2-inch ring mold, pipe the mousse mixture halfway up and push a small scoop of peanut butter ice cream into center. Pipe to fill, tap down, smooth tops and freeze.

For the peanut butter ice cream:
Combine cream, half-n-half and 2/3 cup sugar in stainless heavy bottom pot, bring rapidly to simmer, remove from heat and let stand 5 minutes.

Whisk yolks with 1/3 cup sugar until creamy yellow.

Slowly drizzle hot liquid into egg mixture in stages until well combined and incorporated. Return to medium heat and stir constantly

216

with wooden spoon till custard coats back of spoon (about 165°). Do not boil!

Strain through fine mesh strainer into stainless bowl and whisk in peanut butter.

Set over bowl of ice until completely cool. Process in ice cream machine according to directions.

When nearly set, sprinkle in chopped peanuts, remove from machine and freeze.

To serve:
3 ripe bananas
1/4 cup sugar in the raw
Optional raspberry sauce, chocolate sauce and cocoa powder to garnish

Remove mousse from molds and arrange on garnished plate (if desired).

Slice bananas and arrange in spiral on top of mousse (use additional peanut butter to adhere if desired). Sprinkle bananas with some of the sugar and use brulee torch to melt and caramelize.

Harmony Bread Pudding

Ingredients:

1 lemon
1 lime
24 croissants
1 Tbls cinnamon
1 Tbls nutmeg
2 cups granulated sugar
1 Tbls vanilla
1 cup orange Cointreau
16 egg yolks
2 cups chocolate
2.5 quarts half & half
Water as needed

To prepare:

Preheat oven to 350°.
Zest lemon and orange with box grater.
Cut croissants into one-inch cubes,
Combine all ingredients except croissants and

Harmony Golf Preserve
Harmony, Florida
Kelvin Fitzpatrick, Executive Chef
Serves 4-6

mix well. Add croissant cubes to mixture. Spray a metal baking pan with cooking spray and fill with pudding mixture. Lay parchment paper on top.

Place the pan into a full-size metal hotel pan in preheated oven, and fill larger pan with cold water until the level is one inch below the top of the pan.

Bake for two hours.

Remove smaller pan and cool in refrigerator for 24 hours before serving.

Lemon-Chevre Pudding Cake
With Mango Sauce

Atlantic Room at Kiawah Island Resort
Kiawah Island, South Carolina

Randy MacDonald, Executive Chef
Serves 10

Ingredients:

1 cup granulated sugar
1/3 cup all-purpose flour
Juice of 6 lemons (or ½ cup of lemon juice)
12 Tbls (1½ sticks) unsalted butter, melted
1½ tablespoons lemon zest
9 egg yolks
2¼ cups whole milk
4½ egg whites
4 ounces goat cheese, room temperature
1 tablespoon heavy cream
1 whole egg, beaten
1 teaspoon vanilla extract
4 Tbls unsalted butter, room temperature
1½ pints blackberries

For the Mango Sauce:
3 cups frozen chunks of mango
3 tablespoons honey
Juice from 1 fresh lime

To prepare:

Cream the goat cheese with 2 tablespoons of sugar until creamy. Add the heavy cream and vanilla extract. Beat in the whole eggs a little at a time. Set aside.

Mix ½ cup of the sugar with 1/3 cup of the all purpose flour. Add all of lemon juice, the melted butter, the lemon zest and the egg yolks. Stir in the milk. Stir in the goat cheese batter. Separately, beat the egg whites to stiff peaks. Fold into the batter.

Rub non-stick molds with room temperature butter. Divide the remaining sugar among the 10 cups. Bake at 300° in a water bath until thoroughly cooked (approximately 1 hour). Cool in molds. Invert on a sheet pan. Carefully remove the mold.

Thaw the mango in the microwave. Save the juices. Puree with the honey and the lime juice. Adjust the sweetness with additional honey, if necessary. Strain through a medium strainer.

Top the cakes with washed blackberries to order and serve with Mango Sauce.

219

Peach Bread Pudding

The Verandah Grill at The Partidge Inn
Augusta, Georgia

Bradley Czajka, Executive Chef
Serves 4

Ingredients:

2 ½ pounds day-old croissants, brioche
    and bread
1 quart chopped peaches
½ quart half & half
6 eggs
½ cup sugar
½ tablespoon cinnamon

To prepare:

Cut bread into large chunks and place in stainless steel bowl with chopped peaches.

Whisk together all other ingredients until thoroughly combined.

Place over bread mixture and let soak for at least 15 minutes.

Back in 350° oven for 40 minutes or until golden brown and set in the middle.

Let cool slightly before serving.

Top with sliced peaches and powdered sugar.

220

Pumpkin White Chocolate Creme Brulee

Hendersonville Country Club
Hendersonville, North Carolina

Steve Goodhoe, Executive Chef

Serves 6

Ingredients:

1 ½ cup whipping cream
½ cup half and half
4 Tbls pumpkin puree
¼ tsp pumpkin pie spice
¼ cup white chocolate chips
¼ cup egg yolks
¼ cup granulated sugar
1 tsp vanilla extract
6 tsp light brown sugar (cane sugar works best)

To prepare:

Gently heat cream, half and half, pumpkin puree and pie spice, stirring occasionally until hot. Do not allow to boil. Add white chocolate chips and stir until melted. Remove from heat and strain through a fine sieve to remove pumpkin pulp.

Combine egg yolks, sugar and vanilla and stir until smooth. Slowly add the cream mixture while stirring to prevent lumps.

Divide mixture between six individual crème brulee dishes. Bake on a cookie sheet in a 250° oven until the mixture reaches 165° in the center, or until set. Remove from oven and allow to cool. Refrigerate at least three hours.

Make a thin coat of brown sugar on top of each dish and place in the broiler until the sugar is melted but not burned. Allow to cool and garnish if desired with mint leaves and fresh raspberries or homemade cranberry sauce.

Sabayon

Rosen Shingle Creek Resort
Orlando, Florida

Jorge Oliveira,, Executive Chef
Serves 4

Ingredients:

½ cup Marsala wine
3 tablespoons sugar
5 egg yolks
1 teaspoon gelatin
1 ½ cups heavy cream

To prepare:

Bloom gelatin.

Bring marsala and sugar to a boil. Start whipping eggs and slowly pour mixture down the side of the mixing bowl.

Melt gelatin and add it to marsala mixture. Cool mixture down and add heavy cream.

Store in refrigerator and serve on top of your favorite cake.

Southern White Chocolate Bread Pudding

Daniel Island Club
Charleston, South Carolina
Tyler Dudley, Executive Chef

Ingredients:

16 ounces whole milk
16 ounces heavy cream
2 whole eggs
1 Tbls vanilla
   extract
12 fresh croissants,
   broken
   into pieces
1 ounce Maker's
   Mark bourbon
6 ounces sugar
2 ounces white
   chocolate, broken
   into small pieces

To prepare:

Combine the milk, cream, vanilla extract and half the sugar and bring to a boil.

Whisk the eggs with the remaining sugar and bourbon. Temper the hot liquid slowly into the beaten eggs.

Strain over croissant pieces and white chocolate. Soak for at least 15 minutes.

Pour into greased baking cups. Bake in water bath at 325° until the center is set.

Teresa's Lacy Jumbles

Long Cove Club
Hilton Head Island, South Carolina

Teresa Brandow, Pastry Chef
Yield: 3 logs

Ingredients:

3½ ounces pecan halves
11½ounces unblanched almonds
7½ ounces whole wheat flour
1 1/3 tsp baking powder
Pinch salt
4½ ounces granulated sugar
2½ ounces light brown sugar
10 Tbls (1 1/4 stick)
    butter, unsalted,
    softened at room
    temperature
2½ ounces eggs
½ tsp. vanilla extract
4 ounces semi-sweet
    chocolate chips
4 ounces white
    chocolate chips
10 ounces raisins

Long Cove members love these cookies from pastry chef Teresa Brandow, according to executive chef Leonard Giarratano. They like her macaroons even more ... but she wouldn't share that recipe!

To prepare:

Lightly toast the pecans and almonds.

Preheat oven to 375°.
In a small bowl sift together the flour, baking soda, and salt, whisking together for even distribution.

In a stand mixer, cream the sugars and the butter until light and fluffy. Beat in the egg and vanilla on low speed. Then beat in the flour mixture until well incorporated into a creamy batter.

In a large bowl, mix together the nuts, raisins and chocolate chips.

Empty the batter into the bowl and incorporate the nut mixture.

Using parchment paper, roll into a log about 3.5 inches thick. Chill for at least 2 hours.

When ready to bake, slice into ½" to ¾" cookies and place on parchment lined sheet pan. Bake in a conventional over at 350° for 11 minutes, then rotate once and bake an additional 5 minutes or so until done.

Tropical Clouds
Hammock Bay Golf & Country Club
Naples, Florida

Desmond McGuire, Executive Chef

Ingredients:

4 egg whites
3/4 cup sugar
1 ½ tsp lemon zest
1 cup heavy cream
1 tsp vanilla extract
2 Tbls sugar
1 papaya
1 mango
½ pint straw-
   berries
1 teaspoon
   lemon juice
1 tablespoon
   sugar

Parchment
   paper
Pastry bag with
   star tip

clouds less than ½ inch thick. Bake at 225°
for 1 to 2 hours or until clouds are crisp but
not dry. Let clouds cool and store in tightly
closed plastic bags.

With mixer on high speed beat heavy cream,
2 tablespoons of sugar and the vanilla extract
until soft peaks form. Remove from mixer
and chill until
needed.

Peel and cut
mango into ½
inch pieces. Peel
and cut pa-
paya into ½ inch
pieces. Clean and
slice strawber-
ries. Combine all
fruit, lemon juice
and remaining
sugar and place
in refrigerator
until chilled.

To prepare:
Pre-heat oven to 225°.
Beat egg whites in mixer until foamy with
soft peaks. Add 1/2 cup of the sugar and whip
until egg whites become stiff and glossy. Remove egg whites from mixer and gently fold
in lemon zest and the remaining sugar.

Pipe meringue mixture onto baking sheets
lined with parchment paper. Try to keep

To serve, place a meringue cloud onto a dessert plate and spoon or pipe whipped cream on
top. Gently place chilled fruit with its juices
onto whipped topping. To finish cloud can
be topped with additional whipped cream or
served with pureed mango.

225

Wexford Plantation Lemon Pound Cake

Wexford Plantation
Hilton Head Island, South Carolina
Frank Copeland, Executive Chef

Ingredients:

1 cup Crisco shortening
4 Tbls butter, softened
1 2/3 cups sugar
6 eggs
2 cup flour sifted twice & with a pinch of salt
1 teaspoon vanilla extract
¾ teaspoon lemon extract

To prepare:

Cream butter, shortening and sugar until fluffy and pale white in color with a stand mixer (preferably with a paddle attachment).

Add eggs one at a time until all are incorporated.

On low speed add flour in thirds, scraping bowl with each addition. Add extracts and pour into a bundt cake pan that is buttered and floured.

Bake 325° for 55 minutes or tested done by tooth pick method.

PHOTO COURTESY GROG AT WEXFORD PLANTATION

White Chocolate Mascarpone Cloud
With Marsala Figs

Orchid Island Golf & Beach Club
Vero Beach, Florida

Jeff McKinney, Executive Chef
Yield: 6-8 cups

Ingredients:

For the clouds:
2 cups whipping cream
3 Tbls sugar
1 tsp vanilla extract
½ pound Mascarpone cheese at room temperature
1 cup white chocolate in small pieces

For the figs:
12 dried figs
¼ cup sugar
¼ cup Marsala wine

To prepare:

Whip the first three ingredients until soft peaks form. Set aside.

Melt the white chocolate pieces in a water bath or in the microwave oven, 10 seconds at a time, stirring each time. Do not overheat.

Gently combine with the Mascarpone cheese using a folding motion. Fold in the whipped cream.

Spoon into dishes.

Place the figs, sugar and wine in a food processor and mix together until smooth. Spoon some of the fig mixture atop each cloud, garnish as desired with powdered sugar and mint and serve.

227

Glossary
Terms used in this cookbook

Balsamic Reduction: When you slowly cook balsamic vinegar on the stovetop, it will "reduce"--some of the liquid will cook off, leaving a syrup behind.

Blanching is a cooking term that describes a process of food preparation wherein the food substance, usually a vegetable or fruit, is plunged into boiling water, removed after a brief, timed interval and finally plunged into iced water or placed under cold running water (shocked) to halt the cooking process.

The **bouquet garni** (French for "garnished bouquet") is a bundle of herbs usually tied together with string and mainly used to prepare soup, stock, and various stews. The bouquet is boiled with the other ingredients, but is removed prior to consumption.

Brunoise is a method of food preparation in which the food item is first julienned and then turned 90° and diced again, producing cubes of a side length of about 3 mm on each side or less. Common items to be brunoised are leeks, turnips and carrots.

Butterfly. To split food down the center without cutting all the way through so two pieces can be opened like butterfly wings.

Caramelization or caramelisation is the oxidation of sugar, a process used extensively in cooking for the resulting nutty flavor and brown color. When you are caramelizing sugar, combine it and the water in a heavy-bottomed saucepan or pot and put it over medium heat until the sugar melts. Then, using a pastry brush dipped in water, wash down the sides of the pot so that there are no undissolved bits of sugar. Keep cooking the sugar until it turns to the golden or dark brown you want. This can take a while. Just be patient. Use as your recipe directs. Understand that the darker the color of the caramelized sugar, the more pronounced the caramel flavor will be.

Chiffonade is a cooking technique in which herbs or leafy green vegetables (such as spinach and basil) are cut into long, thin strips. This is generally accomplished by stacking leaves, rolling them tightly, then cutting across the rolled leaves with a sharp knife, producing fine ribbons. The French word means "made of rags" referring to the fabric-like strips that result in this technique.

A **chinoise** (sometimes chinois) is an extremely fine meshed conical sieve used for straining soups and sauces to produce a very smooth texture. It can also be used to dust pastries with a fine layer of powdered sugar. It is often accompanied by a conical wooden dowel used to press soft materials through the strainer and performs a similar function to that of a food mill.

Concasse, from the French 'concasser', to crush or grind, is a cooking term meaning to rough chop any ingredient, usually vegetables. This term is most specifically applied to tomatoes, with tomato concasse being a tomato that has been peeled, seeded (seeds and membranes removed), and chopped to specified dimensions. Specified dimensions can be rough chop, small dice, medium dice, or large dice.

Demi-glace is a rich brown sauce in French cuisine used by itself or as a base for other sauces. The term comes from the French for half-iced as the French word glace used in reference to a sauce means icing or glaze. It is traditionally made by combining equal parts of veal stock and sauce espagnole, the latter being one of the five mother sauces of classical French cuisine, and the mixture is then simmered and reduced by half. It is also sold ready-made in grocery stores.

French Butter (Beurre noisette) tastes like hazelnuts, achieved by melting butter until it turns a golden brown.

A **hotel pan** is similar to a large metal roasting pan. Hotel pans are sometimes called "steam table pans."

Gumbo file powder is a necessity for cooking authentic Cajun cuisine. Quite simply, gumbo file powder is the powdered leaves of the sassafras tree. When ground, they smell somewhat like eucalyptus or juicy fruit gum.

Lucques olives are noted for the attractive, almost crescent moon shape, bright green color, firm flesh and flavor that is reminiscent of butter and hazelnuts. This olive is grown in the Languedoc-Roussillon region of France.

A **mandoline** is a kitchen utensil used for thin slicing and cutting juliennes. It consists of two parallel working surfaces, one of which can be adjusted in height. A food item is slid along the adjustable surface until it reaches a blade mounted on the fixed surface, slicing it and letting it fall.

Mirepoix is the French name for a combination of onions, carrots and celery. Mirepoix, either raw, roasted or sautéed with butter, is the flavor base for a wide number of dishes, such as stocks, soups, stews and sauces. Mirepoix is known as the holy trinity of French cooking.

Mis en place (literally "put in place") is a French phrase defined by the Culinary Institute of America as "everything in place," as in set up. It is used in U.S. kitchens to refer to the ingredients, such as cuts of meat, relishes, sauces, par-cooked items, spices, freshly chopped vegetables, and other components that a cook requires for the menu items that they expect to prepare during their shift.

Quenelle. Traditionally, this term refers to a delicate dumpling made with ingredients of ground or minced meat, poultry, fish or vegetables, which has been seasoned and bound with a paste made with the use of breadcrumbs, eggs, egg yolks, fat, flour, rice or cream.

Ricotta Impastata. This fresh delicate cheese, light as whipped cream has the consistency and delicate flavor of soft sweet butter. It is widely used for ravioli and manicotti fillings as well as for Italian Pastries.

229

Roux (pronounced somewhat like the English word "rue") is a mixture of wheat flour and fat. It is the basis of three of the mother sauces of classical French cooking: sauce béchamel, sauce velouté, and sauce espagnole. Butter, vegetable oils, or lard are common fats used. It is used as a base for gravy, other sauces, soufflés, soups and stews.

A **slurry** is a mixture of cornstarch and cold liquid mixed together until smooth, used to thicken a liquid or sauce. Always dissolve cornstarch in a cold liquid before adding to a hot mixture or the cornstarch will lump. After stirring the slurry into a hot liquid, bring it to a boil and simmer until the mixture thickens.

To **supreme** a citrus fruit is to remove the skin, pith, membranes, and seeds, and to separate its segments. Used as a noun, a supreme can be a wedge of citrus fruit prepared in this way.

Sweat. A synonym for sauté, usually with vegetables such as onion, celery and garlic.

Tasso ham is a specialty of Cajun cuisine. In this case, "ham" is a misnomer, since tasso is not made from the leg of a pig, but the shoulder butt. This cut is typically fatty and has a great deal of flavor. Tasso is not typically eaten on its own, but may be found in dishes ranging from pasta to crab cakes, soup to gravy.

Tuile (French for "tile.") A tuile is a thin, crisp cookie that is placed over a rounded object (like a rolling pin or a mold) while still hot from the oven. Once cooled and stiff, the

Index

231

Coming soon: Delicious recipes from the Finest Golf Clubs in California, Oregon and Washington State
Visit www.golfcookbook.com for details!

Foreword by Annika Sorenstam

GOLF *a la* CARTE®
Recipes from America's Finest Clubs

Volume Two: The Pacific Coast